Juicing

Delicious Smoothie & Juicing Recipes to Lose Weight

(Delicious Juicing Recipes That Help You Lose Weight Naturally Fast and Feel Great)

Charles Benton

Published By **Ryan Princeton**

Charles Benton

All Rights Reserved

Juicing: Delicious Smoothie & Juicing Recipes to Lose Weight (Delicious Juicing Recipes That Help You Lose Weight Naturally Fast and Feel Great)

ISBN 978-1-7772796-2-2

No part of this guidebook shall be reproduced in any form without permission in writing from the publisher except in the case of brief quotations embodied in critical articles or reviews.

Legal & Disclaimer

The information contained in this book is not designed to replace or take the place of any form of medicine or professional medical advice. The information in this book has been provided for educational & entertainment purposes only.

The information contained in this book has been compiled from sources deemed reliable, and it is accurate to the best of the Author's knowledge; however, the Author cannot guarantee its accuracy and validity and cannot be held liable for any errors or omissions. Changes are periodically made to this book. You must consult your doctor or get professional medical advice before using any of the suggested remedies, techniques, or information in this book.

Upon using the information contained in this book, you agree to hold harmless the Author from and against any damages, costs, and expenses, including any legal fees potentially resulting from the application of any of the information provided by this guide. This disclaimer applies to any damages or injury caused by the use and application, whether directly or indirectly, of any advice or information presented, whether for breach of contract, tort, negligence, personal injury, criminal intent, or under any other cause of action.

You agree to accept all risks of using the information presented inside this book. You need to consult a professional medical practitioner in order to ensure you are both able and healthy enough to participate in this program.

Table Of Contents

Chapter 1: Juicing Defined For Beginners. 1

Chapter 2: The Juicing Revolution 8

Chapter 3: The Art Of Juicing 14

Chapter 4: Common Fruits And Vegetables For Juicing 20

Chapter 5: Digestive Health Juice Recipes 31

Chapter 6: Detoxifying Juice Recipes 49

Chapter 7: Weight Loss Juices Recipes ... 69

Chapter 8: Energy Boosting Juices Recipes 101

Chapter 9: Anti Inflammatory Juices Recipes 133

Chapter 10: The Fascinating History 159

Chapter 11: Embracing The Benefits Of Juicing 169

Chapter 12: Essential Tools 176

Chapter 1: Juicing Defined For Beginners

The resource of health-aware people for many years, has gained first rate reputation in modern years. If you're a amateur within the global of juicing, you might be curious approximately what it includes, why it's so well-known, and the way it is able to advantage your health. This complete manual is designed to reply all of your questions and offer you with the vital statistics you need to embark for your juicing adventure.

1. What is Juicing?

At its middle, juicing is the approach of extracting the liquid content material fabric (juice) from cease quit result and vegetables, leaving at the back of the strong pulp. This juice is commonly consumed as a easy beverage, regularly referred to as "smooth juice" or in reality "juice." Juicing can be executed using diverse strategies, which includes a juicer, blender, or perhaps a guide press.

2. The Popularity of Juicing

Juicing has won reputation for numerous compelling reasons:

Nutrient Concentration

One of the primary blessings of juicing is that it permits you to devour a centered source of crucial nutrients decided in culmination and greens. When you juice, you are extracting nutrients, minerals, antioxidants, and phytonutrients from the produce, making them without problems absorbable with the aid of using your frame.

Easy Digestion

The elimination of fiber at some point of juicing manner that your digestive gadget would no longer need to paintings as difficult to approach the nutrients. This may be particularly useful for individuals with digestive issues or those searching out a quick energy increase.

Hydration

Fresh juices are an awesome deliver of hydration, mainly while made with water-rich give up stop result and vegetables like cucumbers, watermelon, and citrus culmination. Staying hydrated is important for common health.

Detoxification

Many humans flip to juicing as a manner to detoxify their our bodies. While clinical evidence supporting detox diets is limited, a few humans find that ingesting nutrient-wealthy juices makes them revel in greater energized and refreshed.

Weight Management

Juicing can be part of a balanced diet plan and might help with weight management. Replacing excessive-calorie, sugary beverages with smooth juices can lessen calorie intake while presenting critical vitamins.

Variety and Taste

Juicing permits you to check with a huge kind of culmination and veggies, growing precise taste mixtures. It's an thrilling manner to contain more produce into your weight loss plan, especially in case you're not eager on consuming excellent end result or vegetables whole.

three. The Basic Equipment

Before diving into juicing, it is vital to apprehend the primary system you will need: Juicer

A juicer is a specialized appliance designed to extract juice from cease result and vegetables at the equal time as keeping aside the pulp.

There are primary varieties of juicers: centrifugal and masticating. Centrifugal juicers are quicker but may additionally additionally produce barely much less juice and generate greater warmth, probably affecting nutrient content cloth. Masticating juicers feature at lower speeds, keeping greater vitamins however usually come at a higher rate.

Blender

A immoderate-tempo blender also can be used for juicing, even though it could not separate the pulp from the juice. Instead, it creates a thick and clean juice known as a "smoothie." Blending maintains the fiber, making it a exceptional preference in case you make a decision upon a thicker beverage with more satiety.

Manual Juicer

A manual juicer, regularly used for citrus fruits like oranges and lemons, calls for physical try and extract juice. It's a finances-first-rate choice for those trying to juice on a smaller scale.

Nut Milk Bag

If you are the use of a blender to make juice or smoothies, a nut milk bag can be used to stress out the pulp and create a smoother consistency.

Glass Bottles or Jars

To shop your sparkling juice, you could want glass bottles or jars with tight-becoming lids. Glass is desired over plastic due to the fact it would now not leach chemical substances into the juice.

four.   Choosing Your Ingredients

Selecting the right elements is crucial to growing scrumptious and nutritious juices. Here are some pointers:

Freshness Matters

Use sparkling, ripe produce for the extraordinary flavor and nutrient content material cloth fabric. Check for any signs and symptoms of spoilage or overripeness.

Variety is Key

Experiment with a number of quit end result and vegetables to make sure a large spectrum of nutrients on your juices. Different shades normally suggest brilliant nutrient profiles.

Organic vs. Conventional

While natural produce is regularly desired for juicing as it's grown with out synthetic pesticides or fertilizers, it isn't always continuously vital. Washing and striping conventional produce can reduce pesticide residues.

Seasonal Choices

Opt for seasonal culmination and veggies to revel in the terrific flavor and potentially decrease expenses. Seasonal produce is also much more likely to be regionally sourced and extra energizing.

Chapter 2: The Juicing Revolution

The Juicing Revolution has reshaped the landscape of health and health, profoundly impacting how humans method nutrients and properly-being. This phenomenon, rooted inside the easy act of extracting juice from clean end result and veggies, has transcended mere dietary fads. It represents a critical shift in our expertise of the electricity of nature's bounty and the exquisite potential of our our our bodies to thrive at the identical time as nourished with herbal, liquid energy.

Historical Roots:

The origins of juicing can be traced again to ancient civilizations wherein people squeezed the life-keeping drinks from various plants for sustenance. However, the present day-day Juicing Revolution simply received momentum inside the latter 1/2 of of the 20 th century. It have emerge as initially championed with the resource of fitness enthusiasts who diagnosed the untapped capability of uncooked, unprocessed produce inside the fight towards persistent illnesses and dietary deficiencies.

The Science of Juicing:

At the coronary heart of the Juicing Revolution lies the technology of extracting critical vitamins, nutrients, minerals, and enzymes from give up result and vegetables in their most targeted shape. This device gives a robust dose of bioavailable nutrients this is without difficulty absorbed through the frame, permitting it to thrive and heal. The hobby that a pitcher of freshly squeezed juice can supply a nutrient-packed punch have come to be a catalyst for alternate inside the manner human beings approached their diets.

Equipment and Innovation:

In this revolution, the standard juicer transformed proper right into a important device. Innovations in juicing generation brought about the development of diverse juicer types, each designed to cater to splendid dreams. The centrifugal juicer, with its rapid spinning blades, made juicing greater available for the hundreds. Meanwhile, masticating juicers, which gently chew through produce, emerged as the choice for the ones seeking out most nutrient maintenance.

Health Benefits:

The Juicing Revolution is underpinned with the beneficial useful resource of its easy fitness benefits. Freshly extracted juices are a treasure trove of antioxidants, vitamins, and minerals, capable of bolstering the immune tool, enhancing digestion, and promoting radiant pores and pores and skin. The exercise has additionally been related to weight management, prolonged electricity degrees, and improved intellectual readability. Many have noted the consolation of continual illnesses via everyday juicing, testifying to its healing potential.

Customization and Diversity:

One of the hallmark functions of the Juicing Revolution is its versatility. Juices can be tailor-made to fit man or woman choices and health dreams. Whether it is a inexperienced juice to detoxify, a colourful fruit medley for a burst of strength, or a creamy nut milk for a fulfilling deal with, the opportunities are infinite. This customization has made juicing an inclusive workout, attractive to a numerous fashion of tastes and dietary necessities.

Juicing for Detoxification:

Detoxification is a cornerstone of the Juicing Revolution. Juices, in particular green concoctions providing kale, spinach, and different detoxifying greens, are lauded for their potential to purge the body of accumulated pollutants. A nicely-planned juice cleanse can rejuvenate the frame, reset consuming behavior, and provide a easy begin to those looking to embark on a more in shape way of life.

Overcoming Challenges:

While the Juicing Revolution has garnered massive acclaim, it isn't with out its worrying conditions. Critics argue that juices lack the dietary fiber observed in entire fruits and veggies, it simply is critical for digestive health. There's moreover the ability for immoderate sugar intake while fruit-heavy juices are consumed in abundance. However, proponents counter those stressful conditions with techniques like incorporating pulp lower once more into the food plan or cautiously balancing fruit and vegetable ratios.

Culinary Creativity:

Juicing isn't limited to an insignificant fitness routine; it is a shape of culinary artistry. The creativity worried in crafting delicious and nutritious juice recipes is a supply of satisfaction for fanatics. From experimenting with wonderful surrender cease end result to infusing juices with herbs and spices, juicing has stepped forward the limits of flavor exploration and culinary innovation.

Chapter 3: The Art Of Juicing

Juicing is some distance greater than a mechanical method of extracting juice from quit end result and vegetables; it's miles an paintings form that desires precision, creativity, and a deep knowledge of the substances at your disposal. In this chapter, we delve into the nuances of the artwork of juicing, exploring the techniques, suggestions, and secrets and strategies and strategies that rework a simple juice right into a masterpiece of flavor and vitamins.

1. Ingredient Selection:

The basis of any extremely good juice lies inside the substances you choose out out. The art work begins at the grocery hold or farmer's marketplace, in which you handpick the most up to date, ripest produce. Select a colorful array of fruits and vegetables, each with its precise taste profile and nutritional blessings. Consider the seasonality of additives for the maximum colorful and eco-aware picks.

2. Flavor Balancing Act:

Creating a harmonious aggregate of flavors is the hallmark of a professional juicer. Each thing need to supplement the others, growing a balanced taste profile. Experiment with sweet, bitter, bitter, and savory factors to find the best mixture. For example, the wonder of apples can offset the earthiness of kale, even as a squeeze of lemon can brighten the overall taste.

three. Texture Matters:

Texture performs a pivotal characteristic within the artwork of juicing. Some determine upon their juices silky-clean, at the same time as others experience a bit of pulp and fiber. The desire is yours. Adjust the settings in your juicer or pick out out precise produce to reap the popular texture. For example, a masticating juicer may additionally produce a thicker juice, on the same time as a centrifugal one also can yield a smoother cease result.

4. Layering Flavors:

Like a painter the use of layers of colour to a canvas, don't forget layering flavors for your juices. Start with a base of hydrating cucumber or crisp celery, upload intensity with leafy vegetables like spinach or kale, and end with a burst of sweetness from carrots, apples, or citrus fruits. This layering approach ensures a complex and thrilling taste experience.

five. Fresh Herbs and Spices:

Elevate your juice creations with the addition of sparkling herbs and spices. A sprig of mint can lend a smooth exceptional, at the same time as a pinch of ginger or a sprint of turmeric introduces a diffused zing and effective anti-inflammatory blessings. Be cautious with spices, as a bit goes an prolonged way, and they might without problem overpower the general flavor.

6. Color and Presentation:

The visible appeal of your juice is an crucial a part of the artistry. Vibrant, jewel-toned juices now not handiest appearance attractive however moreover constitute a wealthy recognition of antioxidants and vitamins. Experiment with unique element combinations to acquire a spectrum of colours. Serve your juices in easy glasses to reveal off their splendor and encourage appreciation of the paintings.

7. Temperature Considerations:

The temperature of your materials can impact the very last forestall cease result. Some select their juice chilled, whilst others revel in it at room temperature. Cooling factors within the refrigerator before juicing can help benefit the popular temperature. Remember that chillier juices also can need a touch of sweetness to stability out the chill.

8. Combining Fruits and Vegetables:

Balancing the splendor of cease end result with the earthiness of veggies is a crucial factor of juicing artistry. Vegetables like cucumber and celery make exquisite impartial bases, allowing the fruity flavors to shine. Be conscious of the sugar content fabric in stop end result, as excessive fruit can flip a healthful juice proper right into a sugary beverage.

9. Experimentation and Innovation:

The art work of juicing encourages experimentation and innovation. Don't be afraid to step out of doors your comfort vicinity and try new materials. Unconventional combinations can yield extensively high-quality outcomes. Keep a magazine to record your experiments, noting which flavors labored properly collectively and which of them did not.

10. Consistency and Creativity:

While consistency on your juicing routine is essential for reaping fitness benefits, creativity continues the paintings of juicing thrilling. Have fun at the side of your creations, and do not be afraid to get innovative. Seasonal produce, vacations, and personal milestones can all inspire unique juice recipes that upload range and pride on your every day every day.

Chapter 4: Common Fruits And Vegetables For Juicing

Juicing is a cute manner to transform nature's bounty into liquid nourishment. Among the myriad options to be had, positive stop result and greens stand out as staples in the global of juicing. In this exploration, we are able to dive into the colourful spectrum of produce, unveiling the suitability and advantages of every difficulty as we embark on a colorful adventure through the orchards and gardens of the juicing universe.

Apples:

Let's start with the ever-well-known apple. Apples are the essential base for lots juice recipes. Their sweet, crisp flavor gives a herbal supply of sugar, making them an remarkable choice for beginners and those with a sweet enamel. Apples additionally upload a clean tartness to juice blends, balancing out the flavors of leafy greens and further robust veggies. Varieties like Fuji, Gala, and Granny Smith provide subtle variations in sweetness and acidity, bearing in mind nuanced taste profiles in your juices.

2. Oranges:

Oranges, with their vibrant orange hue and citrusy zing, are a favorite preference for juicers. Bursting with vitamin C, oranges beautify the immune gadget and add a sparkling tang to juices. Their excessive water content material contributes to a slight and hydrating outstanding, making them best for publish-exercising or summertime refreshment. To maximize flavor, choose out ripe, juicy oranges and consider which includes a sprint of their zest for a further burst of citrusy aroma.

Carrots:

Carrots are a juicing powerhouse, recognized for his or her candy and earthy taste. Their colourful orange shade recommendations on the rich awareness of beta-carotene, a precursor to diet A, which promotes healthy pores and skin and eyes. Carrots aggregate well with diverse quit end result and greens, improving every the taste and dietary price of your juice. Whether juiced on their non-public or blended with wonderful additives, carrots deliver a subtle sweetness and a touch of earthiness to the combination.

Spinach:

The lush inexperienced leaves of spinach are a dietary treasure trove for juicers. Packed with nutrients, minerals, and antioxidants, spinach contributes to conventional health and electricity. Its slight, slightly earthy flavor makes it a incredible green for those new to juicing. Spinach blends seamlessly with culmination like apples and pears, adding a nutrient beautify with out overpowering the surprise of the juice. Its immoderate chlorophyll content material gives your juices a colorful inexperienced colour.

Kale:

Kale, frequently celebrated as a superfood, is a robust green for the adventurous juicer. Its barely sour and peppery notes can be tamed with the proper combos. Kale is rich in nutrients K, A, and C, further to folate and fiber. Combining kale with sweeter give up end result like apples or pineapples and together with a dash of lemon or ginger can help stability its formidable taste profile. The forestall result is a nutrient-dense, inexperienced elixir packed with fitness advantages.

Cucumbers:

Cucumbers deliver a clean and hydrating first rate on your juices. Their immoderate water content material makes them best for developing a mild and rejuvenating beverage. Cucumbers have a moderate, slightly sweet taste that pairs quite with pretty a few components. They also act as a herbal hydrating agent, making them an awesome desire for positioned up-workout or warmness summer season days. Cucumber-primarily based juices are regularly used as a base for cleansing and cleansing recipes.

Ginger:

Ginger is the spice of the juicing international, collectively with warmth and zing to your blends. While it is commonly applied in smaller portions because of its robust taste, ginger gives numerous health blessings. It aids digestion, reduces infection, and offers a exceedingly spiced kick in your juices. When incorporating ginger, start with a small piece and regulate to flavor. It pairs harmoniously with citrus end result, carrots, and vegetables, infusing your juice with a pleasant, invigorating spice.

Berries (Strawberries, Blueberries, Raspberries):

Berries are a colourful and antioxidant-wealthy addition in your juicing repertoire. Strawberries, blueberries, and raspberries offer a burst of sweetness and a brilliant array of colors. They are low in power and excessive in vitamins and minerals, making them a splendid desire for every taste and health. Berries may be juiced on their very non-public or mixed with extraordinary culmination for a berry-infused satisfaction. Their herbal sugars growth the marvel of your juice at the same time as supplying a luscious, fruity aroma.

Celery:

Celery is a slight and hydrating vegetable, making it an superb desire for juicing. Its excessive water content cloth contributes to the liquid quantity of your juice, at the identical time as its subtle, slightly salty taste gives a savory phrase. Celery juice is widely identified for its capability to help digestive fitness and hydration. When incorporating celery, hold in mind mixing it with cucumbers, apples, and a hint of lemon for a smooth, balanced juice.

Beets:

Beets, with their colorful purple hue, deliver a sweet and earthy flavor to the juicing palette. They are loaded with essential vitamins like folate, potassium, and fiber. Beets are often associated with improved blood flow into and persistence, making them a favourite among athletes. When juicing beets, pair them with cease result like apples and citrus to balance their earthiness. Beets are also recognized to stain, so manage them with care to avoid staining your juicer or counter tops.

Pineapples:

Pineapples infuse your juices with tropical flair and a burst of sweetness. Their tangy, tropical flavor pairs nicely with a great variety of factors, from leafy veggies to ginger. Pineapples are rich in nutrients C and bromelain, an enzyme appeared for its anti inflammatory houses. When choosing pineapples for juicing, pick out ones which can be ripe and aromatic to make sure maximum taste and beauty.

12. Lemon:

Lemons are a juicer's secret weapon, able to raising the flavor of any juice. Their vibrant acidity presents a fresh zing and balances the surprise of fruits. Lemons are also rich in diet C and antioxidants, making them a health-boosting detail. A squeeze of lemon juice can enhance the overall taste and aroma of your creations at the same time as inclusive of a hint of citrusy brightness.

Parsley:

Parsley, often used as a garnish, is an unexpected however nutritious addition in your juicing repertoire. It has a clean, grassy flavor that may add intensity for your juice blends. Parsley is full of nutrients K, C, and A, similarly to essential minerals. It pairs properly with citrus culmination and cucumber, contributing a mild herbal be conscious and an infusion of green goodness in your juices.

Watermelon:

Watermelon is a juicy and hydrating fruit it in reality is incredible for juicing on warm summer season days. Its immoderate water content material material contributes to a slight and smooth juice, at the same time as its herbal sweetness makes it an attractive choice. Watermelon is wealthy in vitamins A and C and consists of antioxidants like lycopene, regarded for its capability to sell coronary coronary heart health. When juicing watermelon, take into account such as a dash of lime or mint to enhance its flavor and aroma.

15. Pears:

Pears provide a subtle sweetness and a sensitive aroma that pairs fantastically with a huge sort of additives. They are a first-rate deliver of nutritional fiber, nutrition C, and potassium. Pears are known for their mild, soothing effect at the digestive machine. Combining pears with ginger, apples, or leafy veggies can create a balanced and palatable juice with a touch of pear's particular taste.

Avocado:

Avocado, often related to creamy textures and savory dishes, could possibly marvel you as a juicing difficulty. While not generally juiced on my own, avocado may be combined with special materials to create wealthy and perfect smoothies. Its healthy fat contribute to a creamy consistency, and its mild flavor complements every sweet and savory profiles. Avocado-primarily based juices are not simplest nutritious but additionally satiating, making them a great desire for meal replacements or submit-workout restoration.

Tomatoes:

Tomatoes are a savory twist within the international of juicing. Their rich, umami taste is balanced with the aid of a slight acidity, developing a unique juice revel in. Tomatoes are a treasured source of vitamins A and C, further to lycopene, recognized for its capacity to guide coronary coronary heart health. Tomato-based juices, often seasoned with herbs like basil and a pinch of salt, can be cherished as a savory opportunity to candy fruit juices.

Mint:

Mint is a fragrant herb that gives a smooth and aromatic detail on your juices. It pairs quite well with quit result like watermelon, citrus, and berries, infusing your creations with a fab and invigorating taste. Beyond its brilliant taste, mint is concept for its functionality to appease digestive ache and promote rest. A few clean mint leaves can remodel your juice proper proper right into a revitalizing and fragrant elixir.

Chapter 5: Digestive Health Juice Recipes

1. Soothing Minty Cucumber Cooler

Preparation Period: 10 Min

Serves: 1

Ingredients desired:

1 cucumber, stripped and diced

A handful of sparkling mint leaves

1/2 of lemon, stripped and deseeded

half-inch piece of easy ginger

1 cup whole of water

Preparation way

1. Wash and strip the cucumber. Dice it into small quantities.

2. Strip the lemon and put off any seeds.

3. Add the cucumber, mint leaves, lemon, and ginger to a juicer.

4. Juice the elements, then dilute with water as desired.

five. Serve chilled.

Serving Total:

Kcal: 32

Carbs: 8g

Fat: 0g

Protein: 1g

2. Ginger Turmeric Digestive Elixir

Preparation Period: five Min

Serves: 1

Ingredients needed:

1-inch piece of ginger

1-inch piece of glowing turmeric (or 1/2 of tsp turmeric powder)

half lemon, stripped and deseeded

A pinch of black pepper

1 cup entire of water

Preparation system

1. Strip the ginger and turmeric (if the use of glowing).

2. Remove any seeds from the lemon.

three. Add the ginger, turmeric, lemon, and a pinch of black pepper to a juicer.

four. Juice the elements.

five. Dilute with water as favored.

6. Serve warmth or at room temperature.

Serving Total:

Kcal: 19

Carbs: 5g

Fat: 0g

Protein: zero.5g

3. Papaya and Pineapple Digestive Bliss

Preparation Period: 10 Min

Serves: 2

Ingredients wished:

1 cup complete of ripe papaya, stripped and deseeded

1 cup entire of glowing pineapple chunks

half of lime, stripped and deseeded

A handful of smooth mint leaves

1 cup whole of water

Preparation approach

1. Strip and deseed the papaya.

2. Cut the pineapple into chunks.

3. Strip and deseed the lime.

4. Add the papaya, pineapple, lime, and mint leaves to a juicer.

five. Juice the additives.

6. Dilute with water as preferred.

7. Serve chilled.

Serving Total:

Kcal: 76

Carbs: 20g

Fat: 0g

Protein: 1g

four. Fennel and Pear Digestive Refresher

Preparation Period: 10 Min

Serves: 1

Ingredients favored:

1 medium fennel bulb, trimmed

1 ripe pear, cored

half of lemon, stripped and deseeded

1-inch piece of sparkling ginger

1 cup entire of water

Preparation gadget

1. Trim the fennel bulb and eliminate the hard outer layer.

2. Core the pear.

three. Strip the lemon.

four. Add the fennel, pear, lemon, and ginger to a juicer.

five. Juice the materials.

6. Dilute with water as desired.

7. Serve chilled.

Serving Total:

Kcal: 151

Carbs: 38g

Fat: 0g

Protein: 2g

five. Beet and Carrot Digestive Booster

Preparation Period: 10 Min

Serves: 1

Ingredients wished:

1 medium beet, stripped

2 large carrots, stripped

half of lemon, stripped and deseeded

1-inch piece of glowing ginger

A pinch of crushed cinnamon

Preparation approach

1. Strip the beet and carrots.

2. Strip the lemon and take away any seeds.

3.   Add the beet, carrots, lemon, ginger, and a pinch of cinnamon to a juicer.

4.   Juice the substances.

5.   Serve chilled.

Serving Total:

Kcal: one hundred ninety

Carbs: 45g

Fat: 1g

Protein: 4g

6. Green Apple and Spinach Digestive Delight

Preparation Period: 10 Min

Serves: 1

Ingredients wanted:

2 green apples, cored

2 cups of easy spinach leaves

1/2 of cucumber, stripped

half of lemon, stripped and deseeded

A handful of clean mint leaves

Preparation approach

1. Core the inexperienced apples.

2. Wash the spinach leaves.

three. Strip the cucumber and the lemon.

four. Add the green apples, spinach, cucumber, lemon, and mint leaves to a juicer.

5. Juice the components.

6. Serve chilled.

Serving Total:

Kcal: a hundred seventy five

Carbs: 43g

Fat: 1g

Protein: 3g

7. Ginger and Pineapple Digestive Zing

Preparation Period: 10 Min

Serves: 1

Ingredients wished:

1 cup whole of sparkling pineapple chunks

1-inch piece of easy ginger

half of of lime, stripped and deseeded

A pinch of cayenne pepper (non-compulsory)

1 cup complete of water

Preparation method

1. Cut the pineapple into chunks.

2. Strip the ginger.

3. Strip the lime and cast off any seeds.

four. Add the pineapple, ginger, lime, and a pinch of cayenne pepper (if preferred) to a juicer.

five. Juice the materials.

6. Dilute with water as wanted.

7.   Serve chilled.

Serving Total:

Kcal: 99

Carbs: 26g

Fat: 0g

Protein: 1g

8. Lemon Ginger Mint Digestive Cooler

Preparation Period: 10 Min

Serves: 1

Ingredients preferred:

1 lemon, stripped and deseeded

1-inch piece of smooth ginger

A handful of glowing mint leaves

1/2 cucumber, stripped

1 cup complete of water

Preparation approach

1. Strip the lemon.

2. Strip the ginger.

three. Wash the mint leaves.

4. Strip the cucumber.

five. Add the lemon, ginger, mint leaves, cucumber, and water to a juicer.

6. Juice the additives.

7. Serve chilled.

Serving Total:

Kcal: 29

Carbs: 9g

Fat: 0g

Protein: 1g

nine. Pineapple and Minty Kale Digestive Detox

Preparation Period: 10 Min

Serves: 1

Ingredients wanted:

1 cup full of clean pineapple chunks

A handful of smooth kale leaves

A handful of clean mint leaves

half of of cucumber, stripped

1/2 of lime, stripped and deseeded

Preparation technique

1. Cut the pineapple into chunks.

2. Wash the kale leaves.

3. Wash the mint leaves.

4. Strip the cucumber and lime.

five. Add the pineapple, kale, mint leaves, cucumber, and lime to a juicer.

6. Juice the components.

7. Serve chilled.

Serving Total:

Kcal: 118

Carbs: 30g

Fat: 0g

Protein: 2g

10. Cucumber and Celery Digestive Cleanser

Preparation Period: 10 Min

Serves: 1

Ingredients wanted:

1 cucumber, stripped

2 celery stalks

half lemon, stripped and deseeded

A handful of clean parsley

1 cup whole of water

Preparation technique

1. Strip the cucumber.

2. Wash the celery stalks.

3. Strip the lemon.

4. Wash the parsley.

five. Add the cucumber, celery, lemon, parsley, and water to a juicer.

6. Juice the components.

7. Serve chilled.

Serving Total:

Kcal: 37

Carbs: 9g

Fat: 0g

Protein: 1g

eleven. Mango and Banana Digestive Smoothie

Preparation Period: 10 Min

Serves: 1

Ingredients desired:

1 ripe mango, stripped and pitted

1 ripe banana

1/2 of cup full of simple yogurt (or dairy-free yogurt)

half of lemon, stripped and deseeded

A pinch of overwhelmed cardamom (optionally available)

Preparation manner

1. Strip and pit the mango.

2. Strip the banana.

3. Strip the lemon.

4. Add the mango, banana, yogurt, lemon, and a pinch of cardamom (if desired) to a blender.

five. Blend until smooth.

6. Serve chilled.

Serving Total:

Kcal: 276

Carbs: 68g

Fat: 2g

Protein: 6g

12. Orange and Carrot Digestive Elixir

Preparation Period: 10 Min

Serves: 1

Ingredients desired:

2 oranges, stripped and deseeded

2 carrots, stripped

1/2 of lemon, stripped and deseeded

1-inch piece of easy ginger

Preparation approach

1. Strip the oranges and dispose of any seeds.

2. Strip the carrots.

three. Strip the lemon.

four. Strip the ginger.

5. Add the oranges, carrots, lemon, and ginger to a juicer.

6. Juice the ingredients.

7. Serve chilled.

Serving Total:

Kcal: 189

Carbs: 46g

Fat: 1g

Protein: 4g

thirteen. Kiwi and Spinach Digestive Green Elixir

Preparation Period: 10 Min

Serves: 1

Chapter 6: Detoxifying Juice Recipes

22. Green Goddess Detox Juice

Preparation Period: 10 Min

Serves: 1

Ingredients wished:

2 cups spinach leaves

1 cucumber

2 celery stalks

1 green apple

half of of lemon (stripped)

1-inch piece of ginger

Preparation device

1. Wash all of the factors very well.

2. Cut the cucumber and celery into smaller portions to fit your juicer chute.

3. Core the apple and decrease it into wedges.

four. Strip the lemon.

5. Juice all the components, beginning with the leafy greens.

6. Pour the juice into a tumbler, stir, and experience!

Serving Total:

Kcal: one hundred twenty

Carbs: 30g

Fats: zero.5g

Protein: 3g

23. Carrot Turmeric Cleansing Juice

Preparation Period: 10 Min

Serves: 1

Ingredients wished:

four medium carrots

1-inch piece of smooth turmeric

1 small orange (stripped)

half of lemon (stripped)

Preparation method

1. Scrub the carrots and dice them into smaller quantities.

2. Strip the turmeric and reduce it into smaller chunks.

3. Strip the orange and lemon.

four. Juice all the additives, beginning with the carrots.

5. Mix properly and serve right away.

Serving Total:

Kcal: 100 and fifty

Carbs: 36g

Fats: zero.5g

Protein: 3g

24. Beetroot Detox Elixir

Preparation Period: 10 Min

Serves: 1

Ingredients needed:

1 medium beetroot (stripped)

2 carrots

1 apple

1/2 lemon (stripped)

1-inch piece of ginger

Preparation method

1. Strip and cube the beetroot.

2. Scrub and dice the carrots.

3. Core the apple and cut it into wedges.

4. Strip the lemon.

five. Juice all of the factors, beginning with the beetroot.

6. Stir nicely and revel in!

Serving Total:

Kcal: one hundred and seventy

Carbs: 42g

Fats: zero.5g

Protein: 3g

25. Pineapple Mint Detox Refresher

Preparation Period: 10 Min

Serves: 1

Ingredients wanted:

2 cups whole of glowing pineapple chunks

1/2 cucumber

A handful of clean mint leaves

1/2 of lime (stripped)

Preparation technique

1. Cut the pineapple into chunks.

2. Dice the cucumber.

3. Remove the mint leaves from the stems.

4. Strip the lime.

5. Juice all the elements, beginning with the pineapple.

6. Mix properly and serve chilled.

Serving Total:

Kcal: 130

Carbs: 34g

Fats: 0.5g

Protein: 2g

26. Spinach and Kale Cleanse Juice

Preparation Period: 10 Min

Serves: 1

Ingredients desired:

2 cups whole of spinach leaves

1 cup full of kale leaves

1 cucumber

2 celery stalks

1 green apple

half of lemon (stripped)

Preparation technique

1. Wash all the leafy greens very well.

2. Cut the cucumber and celery into smaller quantities.

three. Core the apple and decrease it into wedges.

four. Strip the lemon.

5. Juice all of the factors, starting with the leafy greens.

6. Stir nicely and serve right now.

Serving Total:

Kcal: a hundred thirty

Carbs: 32g

Fats: 0.5g

Protein: 4g

27. Watermelon Cucumber Cooler

Preparation Period: 10 Min

Serves: 1

Ingredients wanted:

2 cups whole of diced watermelon (seeds eliminated)

half cucumber

half of of of lime (stripped)

A few glowing basil leaves

Preparation way

1. Dice the watermelon and remove any seeds.

2. Cut the cucumber into smaller portions.

three. Strip the lime.

4. Juice all of the additives, beginning with the watermelon.

5. Garnish with clean basil leaves and serve chilled.

Serving Total:

Kcal: 90

Carbs: 23g

Fats: 0.5g

Protein: 2g

28. Lemon-Ginger Cleansing Shot

Preparation Period: 5 Min

Serves: 1

Ingredients desired:

1 lemon (stripped)

1-inch piece of ginger

Preparation way

1. Strip the lemon.

2. Strip the ginger.

three. Juice each components.

four. Serve as a shot or dilute with water for a milder taste.

Serving Total:

Kcal: 20

Carbs: 6g

Fats: zero.5g

Protein: 1g

29. Citrus Detox Blast

Preparation Period: 10 Min

Serves: 1

Ingredients needed:

1 grapefruit (stripped)

2 oranges (stripped)

1 lemon (stripped)

half of of lime (stripped)

1/2 inch piece of smooth turmeric

Preparation method

1. Strip all of the citrus give up result.

2. Strip the turmeric.

3. Juice all the elements, beginning with the grapefruit.

four. Mix well and serve chilled.

Serving Total:

Kcal: 100 and seventy

Carbs: 43g

Fats: 0.5g

Protein: 3g

30. Blueberry Beet Detox Elixir

Preparation Period: 10 Min

Serves: 1

Ingredients wanted:

half of of cup whole of glowing or frozen blueberries

1 small beetroot (stripped)

1 apple

half of lemon (stripped)

1-inch piece of ginger

Preparation approach

1. Wash the blueberries.

2. Strip and dice the beetroot.

three. Core the apple and decrease it into wedges.

4. Strip the lemon.

five. Strip the ginger.

6. Juice all of the components, beginning with the blueberries.

7. Stir well and enjoy!

Serving Total:

Kcal: a hundred and seventy

Carbs: 42g

Fats: 0.5g

Protein: 3g

31. Celery-Parsley Detox Delight

Preparation Period: 10 Min

Serves: 1

Ingredients wanted:

four celery stalks

A handful of easy parsley

1 cucumber

half of lemon (stripped)

Preparation method

1. Wash the celery stalks and cube them.

2. Remove parsley leaves from the stems.

3. Dice the cucumber.

four. Strip the lemon.

5. Juice all of the additives, starting with the celery.

6. Stir well and serve chilled.

Serving Total:

Kcal: 70

Carbs: 18g

Fats: 0.5g

Protein: 2g

32. Ginger-Turmeric Detox Shot

Preparation Period: five Min

Serves: 1

Ingredients wanted:

1-inch piece of ginger

1-inch piece of clean turmeric

A pinch of black pepper (for advanced turmeric absorption)

Preparation manner

1. Strip the ginger and turmeric.

2. Juice each components.

3. Add a pinch of black pepper for prolonged bioavailability of turmeric.

4. Serve as a shot or dilute with water.

Serving Total:

Kcal: 10

Carbs: 2g

Fats: 0g

Protein: 0g

33. Spinach-Cucumber Hydration Boost

Preparation Period: 10 Min

Serves: 1

Ingredients wanted:

2 cups entire of spinach leaves

1 cucumber

1/2 lemon (stripped)

A pinch of sea salt (non-obligatory, for electrolyte balance)

Preparation technique

1. Wash the spinach leaves.

2. Dice the cucumber.

three. Strip the lemon.

4. Juice all of the elements, starting with the spinach.

5. Add a pinch of sea salt if preferred for electrolyte stability.

6. Stir nicely and revel in!

Serving Total:

Kcal: forty

Carbs: 10g

Fats: 0.5g

Protein: 2g

34. Aloe Vera Detox Elixir

Preparation Period: 10 Min

Serves: 1

Ingredients wanted:

2-3 inches of smooth aloe vera leaf (inner gel excellent)

1 cucumber

1 apple

half of of of lemon (stripped)

Preparation manner

Cut open the aloe vera leaf and scoop out the internal gel.

Dice the cucumber.

Core the apple and decrease it into wedges.

Strip the lemon.

Juice all of the additives, beginning with the aloe vera gel.

Stir properly and serve chilled.

Serving Total:

Kcal: 100 twenty

Carbs: 30g

Fats: zero.5g

Protein: 2g

35. Orange-Turmeric Sunrise Detox

Preparation Period: 10 Min

Serves: 1

Ingredients preferred:

2 oranges (stripped)

1-inch piece of sparkling turmeric

1/2 lemon (stripped)

Preparation manner

1. Strip the oranges.

2. Strip the turmeric.

three. Strip the lemon.

4. Juice all of the additives, beginning with the oranges.

five. Mix properly and serve chilled.

Serving Total:

Kcal: one hundred thirty

Carbs: 32g

Fats: zero.5g

Protein: 2g

36. Cranberry-Cilantro Cleansing Juice

Preparation Period: 10 Min

Serves: 1

Ingredients wanted:

1 cup entire of clean cranberries

A handful of glowing cilantro leaves

1 cucumber

half of of lemon (stripped)

Preparation manner

1. Wash the cranberries.

2. Remove cilantro leaves from the stems.

3. Dice the cucumber.

4. Strip the lemon.

5. Juice all the additives, beginning with the cranberries.

Chapter 7: Weight Loss Juices Recipes

forty two. Berry Blast

Preparation Period: five Min

Serves: 1

Ingredients wanted:

1 cup complete of combined berries (strawberries, blueberries, raspberries)

1/2 cup whole of Greek yogurt

half of cup entire of unsweetened almond milk

1 tsp whole of honey (non-obligatory)

Preparation manner

1. Wash the berries.

2. Add berries, Greek yogurt, almond milk, and honey (if preferred) to a blender.

3. Blend until smooth.

four. Pour into a pitcher and serve chilled.

Serving Total:

Kcal: 100 eighty

Carbs: 30g

Fat: 4g

Protein: 10g

40 three. Green smoothie

Preparation Period: 10 Min

Serves: 1

Ingredients needed:

1 cup whole of kale leaves

1 cup whole of spinach leaves

1/2 cucumber, stripped and sliced

1 inexperienced apple, cored and sliced

half of lemon, stripped

Preparation system

1. Wash the kale and spinach leaves thoroughly.

2. Strip and slice the cucumber.

3. Core and slice the green apple.

four. Strip the lemon.

five. Add all materials to a juicer and procedure.

6. Pour into a pitcher and take satisfaction on this colorful inexperienced juice.

Serving Total:

Kcal: a hundred and forty

Carbs: 34g

Fat: 0.5g

Protein: 3g

forty four. Tropical Paradise

Preparation Period: 5 Min

Serves: 1

Ingredients wished:

half of of cup whole of pineapple chunks

1/2 of of cup entire of mango chunks

half of of banana

1/2 of of cup complete of coconut water

Preparation method

1. Strip and cube the pineapple and mango.

2. Strip the banana.

three. Add all components to a blender.

four. Blend till smooth.

5. Pour into a pitcher and transport yourself to a tropical paradise!

Serving Total:

Kcal: 100 and 80

Carbs: 45g

Fat: 1g

Protein: 2g

45. Carrot Spice Delight

Preparation Period: 8 Min

Serves: 1

Ingredients favored:

2 massive carrots, stripped and sliced

1 orange, stripped and segmented

half of-inch piece of ginger, stripped

A pinch of cinnamon (optionally to be had)

Preparation technique

1. Strip and slice the carrots.

2. Strip and section the orange.

three. Strip the ginger.

4. Add all factors to a juicer along aspect a pinch of cinnamon (if desired) and device.

five. Pour into a pitcher and feature fun with the sweet and noticeably spiced pleasure!

Serving Total:

Kcal: a hundred thirty

Carbs: 32g

Fat: 0.5g

Protein: 2g

46. Sweet Green juice

Preparation Period: 7 Min

Serves: 1

Ingredients wanted:

1 green apple, cored and sliced

1 cup whole of kale leaves

half cucumber, stripped and sliced

1/2 lemon, stripped

A handful of smooth mint leaves

Preparation technique

1. Core and slice the green apple.

2. Wash the kale leaves very well.

three. Strip and slice the cucumber.

four. Strip the lemon.

5. Add all materials, which encompass the mint leaves, to a juicer and way.

6. Pour into a tumbler and experience this sweet and fresh green dream!

Serving Total:

Kcal: 100 and twenty

Carbs: 30g

Fat: 0.5g

Protein: 2g

47. Creamy Avocado Bliss

Preparation Period: 5 Min

Serves: 1

Ingredients desired:

1 ripe avocado, stripped and pitted

half banana

1 cup whole of spinach leaves

1/2 cup complete of unsweetened almond milk

Preparation approach

1. Strip and pit the avocado.

2. Strip the banana.

three. Wash the spinach leaves.

four. Add all substances to a blender.

5. Blend until creamy.

6. Pour into a glass and admire the velvety goodness.

Serving Total:

Kcal: 290

Carbs: 30g

Fat: 19g

Protein: 4g

forty eight. Fiery Fat Burner

Preparation Period: 6 Min

Serves: 1

Ingredients wished:

2 cups complete of spinach leaves

1 cucumber, stripped and sliced

1/2 green apple, cored and sliced

half lemon, stripped

1-inch piece of ginger, stripped

A pinch of cayenne pepper (adjust to taste)

Preparation method

1. Wash the spinach leaves thoroughly.

2. Strip and slice the cucumber.

three. Core and slice the inexperienced apple.

four. Strip the lemon and ginger.

5. Add all factors, collectively with a pinch of cayenne pepper (regulate to taste), to a juicer and manner.

6. Pour into a pitcher and consist of the fiery kick of this metabolism-boosting juice!

Serving Total:

Kcal: 120

Carbs: 30g

Fat: zero.5g

Protein: 3g

9. Blueberry Burst

Preparation Period: five Min

Serves: 1

Ingredients desired:

1 cup full of blueberries

half of of cup whole of spinach leaves

1/2 of banana

1/2 cup complete of unsweetened almond milk

Preparation technique

1. Wash the blueberries.

2. Wash the spinach leaves.

three. Strip the banana.

four. Add all materials to a blender.

five. Blend till easy.

6. Pour into a glass and savor the antioxidant-rich burst of taste.

Serving Total:

Kcal: one hundred 90

Carbs: 45g

Fat: 2g

Protein: 3g

50. Carrot Ginger Zing

Preparation Period: 7 Min

Serves: 1

Ingredients wanted:

2 huge carrots, stripped and sliced

1-inch piece of ginger, stripped

1/2 of of orange, stripped and segmented

A pinch of turmeric (non-obligatory)

Preparation method

1. Strip and slice the carrots.

2. Strip the ginger.

3.   Strip and section the orange.

4.   Add all elements, which consist of a pinch of turmeric (if favored), to a juicer and way.

five.   Pour into a pitcher and revel in the zingy mixture!

Serving Total:

Kcal: one hundred

Carbs: 24g

Fat: 0.5g

Protein: 2g

51. Cucumber Lemonade

Preparation Period: five Min

Serves: 1

Ingredients wanted:

1 cucumber, stripped and sliced

1 lemon, stripped

1 tsp whole of honey (optionally available)

1 cup whole of water

Preparation manner

1. Strip and slice the cucumber.

2. Strip the lemon.

three. Add cucumber, lemon, honey (if desired), and water to a blender.

four. Blend till you've got a clean cucumber lemonade.

five. Pour into a glass and live hydrated with this citrusy concoction!

Serving Total:

Kcal: 35

Carbs: 9g

Fat: zero.5g

Protein: 1g

fifty two. Spinach Pineapple Paradise

Preparation Period: five Min

Serves: 1

Ingredients wanted:

1 cup complete of spinach leaves

half of of of cup entire of pineapple chunks

half of banana

half of of cup whole of coconut water

Preparation technique

1. Wash the spinach leaves.

2. Dice the pineapple into chunks.

three. Strip the banana.

four. Add all additives to a blender.

5. Blend till you have a tropical paradise in a glass.

6. Pour into a pitcher and function amusing with the inexperienced and fruity pleasure.

Serving Total:

Kcal: one hundred forty

Carbs: 33g

Fat: 0.5g

Protein: 2g

fifty 3. Berry Green juice

Preparation Period: 7 Min

Serves: 1

Ingredients desired:

1 cup entire of blended berries (strawberries, blueberries, raspberries)

1 cup entire of spinach leaves

1/2 of cucumber, stripped and sliced

1/2 of lemon, stripped

Preparation gadget

1. Wash the combined berries.

2. Wash the spinach leaves.

three. Strip and slice the cucumber.

4. Strip the lemon.

5. Add all components to a juicer and method.

6. Pour into a pitcher and savour the nutritional powerhouse of berries and greens.

Serving Total:

Kcal: a hundred and forty

Carbs: 34g

Fat: 0.5g

Protein: 3g

54. Spicy Tomato Tango

Preparation Period: 6 Min

Serves: 1

Ingredients wanted:

2 large tomatoes

1/2 cucumber, stripped and sliced

1/2 of bell pepper, seeded and sliced

1/2 of of lemon, stripped

A pinch of cayenne pepper (adjust to flavor)

Preparation manner

1. Wash the tomatoes.

2. Strip and slice the cucumber.

three. Slice the bell pepper, eliminating the seeds.

4. Strip the lemon.

five. Add all materials, which includes a pinch of cayenne pepper (modify to taste), to a juicer and device.

6. Pour into a glass and enjoy this highly spiced tomato tango!

Serving Total:

Kcal: 80

Carbs: 20g

Fat: 0.5g

Protein: 3g

fifty 5. Mango Tango

Preparation Period: five Min

Serves: 1

Ingredients wanted:

1 cup whole of mango chunks

half of cup whole of Greek yogurt

half cup full of coconut water

1 tsp complete of honey (optionally to be had)

Preparation machine

1. Dice the mango into chunks.

2. Add mango chunks, Greek yogurt, coconut water, and honey (if preferred) to a blender.

three. Blend until you've got a creamy and tropical mango tango.

four. Pour into a tumbler and take pleasure in this exceptional deal with!

Serving Total:

Kcal: 220

Carbs: 48g

Fat: 2.5g

Protein: 7g

fifty six. Beet Berry Bliss

Preparation Period: 8 Min

Serves: 1

Ingredients desired:

1 small beet, stripped and sliced

1 cup full of mixed berries (strawberries, blueberries, raspberries)

half of lemon, stripped

1 tsp full of honey (non-obligatory)

Preparation approach

1. Strip and slice the small beet.

2. Wash the blended berries.

three. Strip the lemon.

four. Add beet slices, combined berries, lemon, and honey (if desired) to a juicer and device.

5. Pour into a pitcher and satisfaction inside the earthy sweetness of this beet berry bliss!

Serving Total:

Kcal: a hundred fifty

Carbs: 38g

Fat: zero.5g

Protein: 2g

57. Beet and Carrot Juice

Preparation Period: 15 Min

Serves: 2

Ingredients favored:

2 medium beets, stripped and diced

four medium carrots, stripped and diced

2 apples, cored and sliced

1 lemon, stripped and seeded

1-inch piece of ginger, stripped

1/2 of cup water (non-obligatory, for favored consistency)

Preparation device

1. Strip and dice the beets and carrots.

2. Core and slice the apples.

3. Strip the lemon and cast off any seeds.

four. Strip the ginger.

five. Using a amazing juicer, add the beets, carrots, apples, lemon, and ginger in batches.

6. If you decide on a thinner consistency, add water and mix.

7. Serve right now with a beet slice for garnish.

Serving Total:

Kcal: one hundred fifty

Carbs: 38g

Fat: 0.6g

Protein: 2.5g

58. Spicy Green Metabolism Booster Juice

Preparation Period: 10 Min

Serves: 2

Ingredients desired:

2 cups whole of kale leaves, washed and stems removed

2 inexperienced apples, cored and sliced

1 cucumber, stripped and diced

1 lemon, stripped and seeded

1-inch piece of ginger, stripped

1/2tsp. Complete ofcayenne pepper

1/2 of cup whole of water (optionally available, for preferred consistency)

Preparation system

1. Wash the kale leaves thoroughly, eliminate any hard stems, and set aside.

2. Core and slice the inexperienced apples.

3. Strip and dice the cucumber.

four. Strip the lemon and dispose of any seeds.

five. Strip the ginger.

6. Using a fantastic juicer, add the kale, inexperienced apples, cucumber, lemon, and ginger in batches.

7. Add the cayenne pepper for an extra metabolism improve.

eight. If you pick out a thinner consistency, upload water and blend.

nine. Serve immediately with a lemon wedge.

Serving Total:

Kcal: one hundred forty

Carbs: 37g

Fat: zero.8g

Protein: 3g

fifty nine. Almond Butter Juice

Preparation Period: 10 Min

Serves: 1

Ingredients wished:

2 medium carrots, stripped and sliced

1 small apple, cored and sliced

1/four cup entire of unsweetened almond butter

half of cup complete of water

1tsp. Complete ofof cinnamon powder (non-compulsory for taste)

half of scoop complete of of your preferred plant-based totally protein powder (non-compulsory)

Preparation approach

1. Strip and slice the carrots.

2. Core and slice the apple.

3. In a blender, integrate the sliced carrots, apple slices, almond butter, water, and cinnamon powder (if the use of).

four. Blend till you have got were given a clean, creamy juice.

five. If you want a in addition protein beautify, add your plant-based absolutely protein powder and mix all over again till nicely blended.

6. Pour into a tumbler and get satisfaction from the creamy, protein-packed goodness.

Serving Total:

Kcal: 3 hundred

Carbs: 37g

Fats: 17g

Proteins: 12g

60. Refreshing Amla (Indian Gooseberry) Juice

Preparation Period: 15 Min

Serves: 2

Ingredients wanted:

four-five smooth Amla (Indian Gooseberries)

1-2 tbsp. Full of honey or sugar (modify to flavor)

A pinch of black salt or regular salt (non-compulsory)

1/2 cup complete water (for mixing)

Preparation manner

1. Start with the beneficial aid of selecting smooth, company Amla. Look for culmination which are clean, inexperienced, and free from blemishes. Freshness is essential to getting the nice taste and nutritional value.

2. Rinse the Amla thoroughly below strolling water.Use a clean kitchen towel to pat them dry.

3. Place the Amla on a slicing board.

4. Take every Amla and use a sharp knife to make a shallow lessen spherical its circumference, growing a groove.

5. Gently maintain the Amla at each ends and twist it. The pores and pores and skin have to come off with out problem alongside the groove.

6. Discard the strip. Repeat this machine for all the Amla.

7. Once stripped, slice the Amla in 1/2 of vertically.

eight. Remove any seeds you may find inside the center the use of the prevent of your knife.

nine. Now, reduce the Amla into smaller portions for easy blending.

10. Place the Amla quantities in a blender.

11. Add half a cup complete of water to help with the mixing method.

12. Blend till you benefit a smooth, thick paste.

13. Place a exquisite-mesh strainer or cheesecloth over a bowl or jug.

14. Pour the blended Amla mixture into the strainer to separate the juice from the pulp.

15. Use a spoon to press the pulp and extract as plenty juice as viable.

sixteen.

17. Return the strained Amla juice to the blender. Add 1-2 tbsp. Complete of of honey or sugar, adjusting the splendor for your flavor desire.

18. If preferred, upload a pinch of black salt or regular salt for a subtle savory evaluation (optionally available).

19. Blend in short to contain the sweetener and salt into the juice.

20. Transfer the Amla juice to a pitcher or serving jug.

21. You can serve it right now over ice for a clean drink.

22. Alternatively, refrigerate it for an hour or for a cooler, greater clean experience.

Seving Total:

Kcal: sixty five

Carbs: 16 g

Fats: zero.Eight g

Proteins: zero.6g

sixty one. Leek and Broccoli Juice

Preparation Period: 15 Min

Serves: 2

Ingredients wished:

2 massive leeks, white and moderate inexperienced additives satisfactory

2 cups of glowing broccoli florets

2 apples (e.G., Granny Smith), cored and sliced

1 cucumber, stripped and sliced

1 lemon, stripped and seeded

1-inch piece of glowing ginger, stripped

half of cup complete of clean parsley leaves

Ice cubes (optionally available, for serving)

Preparation method

1. Begin with the aid of thoroughly washing all the veggies and cease quit end result. Trim the tough, darkish inexperienced leaves from the leeks, leaving quality the white and moderate inexperienced additives. Cut the leeks into smaller portions, and set them apart. Cut the cucumber, apples, and lemon into slices, and strip and slice the ginger.

2. Fill a massive pot with water and convey it to a boil. Prepare a bowl of ice water on the facet. Blanch the broccoli florets with the beneficial useful resource of inclusive of them to the boiling water for about 2 Min until they flip top notch green. Quickly transfer them to the ice water to halt the cooking way and maintain their colorful color. Drain and set aside.

3. Set up your juicer consistent with the manufacturer's instructions. Make positive it's miles easy and organized for use.

Chapter 8: Energy Boosting Juices Recipes

sixty. Beetroot and Carrot Power Punch:

Preparation Period: 15 Min

Serves: 1

Ingredients wished:

1 medium beetroot, stripped and diced

2 carrots, stripped and sliced

1 orange, stripped and segmented

1-inch piece of easy ginger

Preparation manner

1. Strip and cube the beetroot and carrots.

2. Strip the orange and section it.

three. Strip the ginger.

4. Combine all the substances in a juicer.

5. Juice until properly combined.

6. Pour into a tumbler and serve.

Serving Total:

Kcal: one hundred and fifty

Carbs: 36g

Fat: 0.5g

Protein: 3g

sixty three. Kale and Banana Energizer:

Preparation Period: 15 Min

Serves: 1

Ingredients wanted:

2 cups of kale leaves (stems eliminated)

1 banana

half green apple, cored and sliced

half of of cup whole of almond milk

Preparation machine

1. Wash the kale leaves thoroughly.

2. Slice the banana.

three. Slice the green apple and dispose of the center.

four. Combine the kale leaves, banana, green apple, and almond milk in a blender.

five. Blend until clean.

6. Pour into a pitcher and experience.

Serving Total:

Kcal: 230

Carbs: 56g

Fat: 2g

Protein: 4g

sixty 4. Ginger Spice. Energy Elixir:

Preparation Period: 10 Min

Serves: 1

Ingredients needed:

1 apple, cored and sliced

1-inch piece of easy ginger

half of of lemon, stripped

A pinch of cayenne pepper (optionally to be had)

Preparation way

1. Slice the apple and eliminate the center.

2. Strip the ginger.

three. Strip the lemon.

4. Combine the apple, ginger, lemon, and a pinch of cayenne pepper (if favored) in a juicer.

five. Juice till well combined.

6. Pour into a pitcher and serve.

Serving Total:

Kcal: ninety

Carbs: 24g

Fat: 0.5g

Protein: 1g

sixty five. Carrot and Turmeric Booster:

Preparation Period: 15 Min

Serves: 1

Ingredients needed:

2 large carrots, stripped and sliced

1 orange, stripped and segmented

1-inch piece of sparkling turmeric

A small piece of easy ginger

Preparation device

1. Strip and slice the carrots.

2. Strip and phase the orange.

three. Strip the turmeric and ginger.

four. Combine all the substances in a juicer.

five. Juice until nicely mixed.

6. Pour into a tumbler and serve.

Serving Total:

Kcal: a hundred

Carbs: 25g

Fat: zero.5g

Protein: 2g

66. Blueberry and Spinach Vitality Blend:

Preparation Period: 10 Min

Serves: 1

Ingredients wanted:

1 cup entire of glowing blueberries

2 cups of spinach leaves

1/2 banana

half cup complete of almond milk

1 tsp of honey (non-compulsory)

Preparation method

1. Wash the blueberries and spinach leaves.

2. Slice the banana.

three. Combine the blueberries, spinach, banana, almond milk, and honey (if preferred) in a blender.

four. Blend till easy.

five. Pour into a pitcher and serve.

Serving Total:

Kcal: 2 hundred

Carbs: 47g

Fat: 2g

Protein: 5g

sixty seven. Mango Madness Energizer:

Preparation Period: 10 Min

Serves: 1

Ingredients wanted:

1 ripe mango, stripped and diced

half cup complete of pineapple chunks

half of banana

1/2 cup whole of coconut water

Preparation way

1. Strip and dice the ripe mango.

2. Cut the pineapple into chunks.

3. Slice the banana.

4. Combine the mango, pineapple, banana, and coconut water in a blender.

five. Blend until creamy.

6. Pour into a tumbler and experience.

Serving Total:

Kcal: 220

Carbs: 54g

Fat: 1g

Protein: 3g

68. Sweet Potato Powerhouse:

Preparation Period: 15 Min

Serves: 1

Ingredients desired:

1 medium candy potato, stripped and diced

1 apple, cored and sliced

half of of orange, stripped and segmented

A pinch of cinnamon (optionally available)

Preparation method

1. Strip and cube the sweet potato.

2. Slice the apple and take away the middle.

three. Strip and phase the orange.

four. Combine the candy potato, apple, orange segments, and a pinch of cinnamon (if desired) in a juicer.

5. Juice till smooth.

6. Pour into a pitcher and serve.

Serving Total:

Kcal: 100 90

Carbs: 48g

Fat: 0.5g

Protein: 2g

sixty nine. Pomegranate Power Punch:

Preparation Period: 10 Min

Serves: 1

Ingredients preferred:

1 cup entire of pomegranate seeds

1 apple, cored and sliced

1/2 lemon, stripped

A handful of easy mint leaves

Preparation approach

1. Extract the pomegranate seeds.

2. Slice the apple and dispose of the middle.

3. Strip the lemon.

four. Wash the smooth mint leaves.

5. Combine all the elements in a juicer.

6. Juice until properly mixed.

7. Pour into a tumbler, garnish with a spray of smooth mint, and serve.

Serving Total:

Kcal: 100 and seventy

Carbs: 43g

Fat: 0.5g

Protein: 2g

70. Spinach and Mango Revitalizer:

Preparation Period: 10 Min

Serves: 1

Ingredients wanted:

2 cups of spinach leaves

1 ripe mango, stripped and diced

1/2 banana

half of cup whole of coconut water

Preparation method

1. Wash the spinach leaves very well.

2. Dice the ripe mango.

three. Slice the banana.

four. Combine the spinach leaves, mango, banana, and coconut water in a blender.

5. Blend until smooth.

6. Pour into a pitcher and serve chilled.

Serving Total:

Kcal: 210

Carbs: 50g

Fat: 1g

Protein: 4g

71. Cherry and Almond Energizer:

Preparation Period: 10 Min

Serves: 1

Ingredients wanted:

1 cup entire of easy cherries, pitted

half cup complete of almonds, soaked and stripped

half of banana

half of cup complete of almond milk

A drizzle of honey (non-obligatory)

Preparation process

1. Pit the glowing cherries.

2. Soak the almonds in water and strip them.

3. Slice the banana.

4. Combine the pitted cherries, soaked almonds, banana, almond milk, and honey (if preferred) in a blender.

5. Blend until creamy.

6. Pour into a pitcher and experience.

Serving Total:

Kcal: 280

Carbs: 40g

Fat: 12g

Protein: 6g

seventy two. Pear and Walnut Energizer:

Preparation Period: 10 Min

Serves: 1

Ingredients wanted:

2 ripe pears, cored and sliced

half of cup whole of walnuts

half of of banana

half of cup entire of almond milk

A pinch of cinnamon (elective)

Preparation method

1. Slice the ripe pears and eliminate the cores.

2. Combine the sliced pears, walnuts, banana, almond milk, and a pinch of cinnamon (if favored) in a blender.

three. Blend until easy.

four.   Pour into a tumbler and serve.

Serving Total:

Kcal: 340

Carbs: 60g

Fat: 15g

Protein: 6g

seventy three. Papaya and Mint Refresher:

Preparation Period: 10 Min

Serves: 1

Ingredients needed:

1 cup complete of clean papaya chunks

half of of cucumber

half of of lime, stripped

A handful of sparkling mint leaves

Preparation technique

1.   Cut the papaya into chunks.

2. Slice the cucumber.

three. Strip the lime.

4. Wash the glowing mint leaves.

five. Combine all the substances in a juicer.

6. Juice until nicely blended.

7. Pour into a tumbler and garnish with a twig of sparkling mint.

Serving Total:

Kcal: a hundred and ten

Carbs: 28g

Fat: 0.5g

Protein: 2g

seventy 4. Banana and Oatmeal Energy Shake:

Preparation Period: 10 Min

Serves: 1

Ingredients wished:

1 banana

1/2 cup whole of rolled oats

half cup complete of Greek yogurt

half of cup entire of almond milk

A drizzle of maple syrup (non-compulsory)

Preparation manner

1. Slice the banana.

2. Combine the banana, rolled oats, Greek yogurt, almond milk, and maple syrup (if desired) in a blender.

3. Blend until clean and creamy.

four. Pour into a tumbler and experience.

Serving Total:

Kcal: 330

Carbs: 60g

Fat: 4g

Protein: 14g

seventy five. Dragon Fruit Energizer:

Preparation Period: 10 Min

Serves: 1

Ingredients needed:

1 dragon fruit, stripped and diced

1/2 cup entire of coconut water

half of lime, stripped

A sprinkle of chia seeds (non-obligatory)

Preparation device

1. Strip and cube the dragon fruit.

2. Strip the lime.

3. Combine the dragon fruit, coconut water, and stripped lime in a blender.

4. Blend till easy.

5. Pour into a tumbler and sprinkle with chia seeds (if favored).

Serving Total:

Kcal: one hundred thirty

Carbs: 32g

Fat: zero.5g

Protein: 2g

seventy six. Kiwi Fruit, Lemon, and Lettuce Juice

Preparation Period: 10 Min

Serves: 2

Ingredients wanted:

4 ripe kiwi fruits

1 lemon

four-five huge lettuce leaves (romaine or green leaf lettuce)

1 cup complete of cold water (optionally available)

Ice cubes (optionally to be had)

Honey or agave nectar (non-obligatory, for brought sweetness)

Preparation manner

1. Wash the kiwi fruits, lemon, and lettuce leaves thoroughly under strolling water.

2. Strip the kiwi culmination. To try this, reduce off the ends of every kiwi, then use a spoon to gently slide under the pores and pores and skin and lift it away from the flesh. Once stripped, slice the kiwi give up end end result into smaller pieces.

3. Roll the lemon on a countertop with the palm of your hand to launch its juices. Cut the lemon in half of of.

four. Set up your juicer regular with the producer's instructions.

five. Begin by feeding the kiwi fruit slices via the juicer chute. Use the plunger to ensure all of the kiwi juice is extracted.

6. Follow through juicing the lemon halves. If your juicer lets in, you may depart the strip on as it consists of critical oils that add taste. However, in case making a decision upon a milder flavor, you may do away with the strip earlier than juicing.

7. Lastly, pass the lettuce leaves via the juicer. The high water content material of lettuce will help extract the flavors from the opportunity elements.

8. If you preference a thinner consistency, you could add a cup complete of cold water and preserve juicing. Adjust the water amount primarily based for your preference for thickness.

9. If you pick a touch of sweetness, you can add honey or agave nectar to the juice and stir until it's far honestly incorporated. Start with atsp. Full ofand upload extra to flavor.

10. Fill glasses with ice cubes, if preferred, for a fresh contact.

eleven.   Pour the freshly prepared juice into the glasses.

12.   Garnish with a kiwi slice or a lemon twist for an elegant presentation.

13.   Sip and delight inside the invigorating flavors of this Kiwi, Lemon, and Lettuce Juice.

Serving Total:

Kcal: 70

Carbs: 18g

Fat: zero.5g

Protein: 2g

77. Berry and Oats Juice: A Nutrient-Rich Morning Elixir

Preparation Period: 10 Min

Serves: 2

Ingredients wished:

For the Juice:

1 cup entire of combined berries (blueberries, strawberries, raspberries, or any of your choice)

half of of cup whole of rolled oats

1 ripe banana

1 cup full of unsweetened almond milk (or any milk of your choice)

half of cup Greek yogurt (non-obligatory for added creaminess)

1 tbsp complete of honey (non-obligatory, for sweetness)

Ice cubes (optionally to be had)

For Garnish:

Fresh berries (for garnish)

A few mint leaves (for garnish)

Preparation manner

1. Gather all of your elements.

2. Rinse the blended berries under bloodless water and pat them dry with a paper towel.

3. Strip the ripe banana and destroy it into smaller chunks.

four. If you're the usage of Greek yogurt, degree it out.

five. Prepare a blender or juicer. Ensure it's easy and prepared to be used.

6. Have ice cubes handy if you decide upon your juice chilled.

7. Start through such as the rolled oats to the blender. This will assist harm them down more effectively.

eight. Follow with the blended berries, banana chunks, and Greek yogurt (if the use of).

nine. If you need to sweeten the juice, add a tablespoon of honey at this stage.

10. Pour in the unsweetened almond milk to make sure the whole thing blends easily.

11. If you choose your juice extra bloodless, throw in a few ice cubes.

12. Cover the blender and blend on immoderate until the combination becomes easy and creamy. This need to take about 2-three Min. If the aggregate is genuinely too thick, you can upload greater almond milk to accumulate your favored consistency.

thirteen. Once the berry and oats juice is silky-easy and properly-combined, it is time to serve.

14. Pour the juice into glasses. You can run the combination through a outstanding strainer in case you pick out a smoother texture, no matter the truth that this step is optionally available.

15. Garnish the glasses with glowing berries of your desire and a few mint leaves for a burst of shade and flavor.

Serving Total:

Kcal: 228

Carbs: 52g

Proteins: 8.5g

Fats: 3.8g

78. Refreshing Watermelon, Kiwi, and Lime Juice Recipe

Preparation Period: 15 Min

Serves: 2

Ingredients desired:

2 cups of diced watermelon (about 1/four of a medium-sized watermelon)

2 ripe kiwis, stripped and diced

2 limes, juiced

1 tablespoon of honey (optionally to be had, regulate to taste)

Ice cubes (elective)

Mint leaves for garnish (non-compulsory)

Preparation technique

1. Preparation: Start with the resource of getting equipped your substances. Wash the watermelon very well, cut it in half, and scoop out the flesh. Cut the watermelon into small cubes, eliminating any seeds along the way. Set aside.

2. Strip and Dice Kiwis: To prepare the kiwis, lessen off every ends of each kiwi fruit. With a knife, carefully strip away the pores and skin. Once stripped, cube the kiwis into small pieces and set apart.

three. Juice the Limes: Roll the limes on a countertop to persuade them to juicier. Cut every lime in 1/2 and juice them the use of a citrus juicer or a fork. Ensure you get rid of any seeds or pulp from the juice.

four. Blend the Ingredients favored: In a blender, combine the diced watermelon, kiwi portions, and freshly squeezed lime juice. If you make a decision in your juice to be a chunk sweeter, you can add a tablespoon of honey at this diploma. The sweetness can be adjusted in line with your flavor. Blend until the combination is smooth and well combined.

five. Strain (Optional): If you want a smoother, pulp-loose juice, strain the mixture through a great-mesh sieve proper right right into a large bowl or pitcher. Use a spoon to softly press the pulp and extract as an awful lot juice as feasible.

6. Chill and Serve: Refrigerate the juice for approximately 30 Min to loosen up it. You can also upload ice cubes straight away to the glasses in advance than pouring the juice. This step is non-obligatory but makes the juice extra smooth, specifically on a heat day.

7. Garnish and Serve: Before serving, garnish your watermelon, kiwi, and lime juice with a twig of easy mint. The mint no longer handiest offers a burst of coloration but additionally enhances the flavors relatively.

Serving Total:

Kcal: eighty 5

Carbs: 22 g

Fat: zero.Five g

Protein: 1 g

79. Carrot and Apple Zinger Recipe

Preparation Period: Approximately 15 Min

Serves: 2

Ingredients preferred:

four medium carrots, washed, stripped, and trimmed

2 apples (ideally sweet kinds like Fuji or Gala), cored and quartered

1 small piece of sparkling ginger (about 1 inch in size), stripped

1 lemon, stripped and seeds eliminated

Ice cubes (non-obligatory, for serving)

Preparation technique

1. Wash, strip, and trim the carrots. Using a vegetable striper or a knife, get rid of the outer pores and skin, and reduce them into smaller quantities to fit your juicer's chute.

2. Core and region the apples, making sure you take away any seeds and stems.

3. Strip the small piece of ginger. If making a decision on a milder ginger taste, you can use much less ginger or adjust it to your taste.

four. Strip the lemon, getting rid of each the zest and the white pith to move away simplest the juicy flesh. Make superb to do away with any seeds.

five. Assemble your juicer regular with the producer's instructions. Ensure it's clean and ready to be used.

6. Start through manner of juicing the carrots. Feed the carrot quantities into the juicer's chute separately, using the plunger to

push them down if essential. Allow the juicer to extract all the liquid from the carrots.

7. Follow through juicing the apple quarters. The sweetness of apples will supplement the earthy taste of carrots.

8. Insert the small piece of stripped ginger into the juicer. Ginger will upload a zing and subtle spiciness on your juice.

9. Finish via way of juicing the stripped lemon. The lemon's tangy flavor will balance the beauty of the apples and carrots, growing a zesty zinger.

10. Once all of the materials are juiced, give the combination a slight stir to mix the flavors thoroughly.

11. You can serve the Carrot and Apple Zinger immediately over ice cubes for a easy, chilled experience.

Chapter 9: Anti Inflammatory Juices Recipes

80 . Parsley, Spinach, and Ginger Juice

Preparation Period: 15 Min

Serves: 2

Ingredients desired:

1 cup complete of clean parsley leaves

2 cups complete of glowing spinach leaves

1-inch piece of sparkling ginger

1 lemon (non-obligatory, for brought flavor)

2-three ice cubes (non-compulsory, for a smooth lighten up)

Preparation gadget

1. Start via manner of thoroughly washing the parsley and spinach underneath cold on foot water to put off any dust or particles. Gently pat them dry with a easy kitchen towel or paper towels.

2. Using a vegetable striper or the brink of a spoon, strip the ginger to remove the outer pores and skin. This will make the ginger much less complex to juice and contribute to a smoother texture inside the very last drink.

three. Cut the lemon in half of and eliminate any seeds. Cut the ginger into smaller pieces to make sure it blends nicely in the juicer.

four. Set up your juicer in step with the producer's instructions. Most juicers require you to area a set subject underneath the spout to seize the juice and a separate discipline for the pulp.

five. To optimize the juicing tool and taste, layer the materials within the juicer as follows; Start with a handful of spinach leaves.Add a small piece of ginger.Follow with a handful of parsley leaves.If the usage of, squeeze the juice from the lemon halves into the juicer.

6. Turn at the juicer and begin the juicing device. Push the elements through the device, permitting it to extract the colourful green juice. Continue juicing till all of the components had been processed.

7. If you pick out your juice chilled, you can add a few ice cubes to the glass or container wherein you advocate to serve the juice.

eight. Pour the freshly extracted juice into glasses. You can stress the juice via a first rate mesh strainer if you select a smoother texture, however this step is elective.

Serving Total:

Kcal: forty-50

Carbs: eleven g

Fats: 0.7 g

Proteins: 2.6 g

80 three. Spinach Berry Juice: A Nutrient-Packed Elixir

Preparation Period: 15 Min

Serves: 2

Ingredients desired:

2 cups entire of sparkling spinach leaves, washed and stems eliminated

1 cup whole of glowing strawberries, hulled and halved

1/2 of cup complete of sparkling blueberries

1 small cucumber, stripped and diced

1 medium inexperienced apple, cored and diced

1 lemon, stripped and quartered

1-inch piece of glowing ginger, stripped

half of cup whole of water (optionally to be had, for preferred consistency)

Ice cubes (non-compulsory, for serving)

Preparation technique

1. Begin with the resource of way of thoroughly washing the spinach leaves and getting rid of any tough stems.

2. Hull the strawberries and reduce them in half.

three. Wash the blueberries and set them aside.

4. Strip the cucumber and cube it into smaller pieces.

5. Core the inexperienced apple and cube it into chunks.

6. Strip the lemon, making sure you do away with all of the zest, and decrease it into quarters.

7. Strip the glowing ginger, which can be effortlessly finished the use of a spoon to scrape off the pores and skin.

8. Set up your juicer in keeping with the manufacturer's instructions, making sure it is smooth and prepared for use.

9. Begin via way of alternating some of the spinach leaves and the opportunity components to make sure an remarkable distribution of flavors and vitamins.

10. Start with a handful of spinach, decided with the useful resource of a few strawberry halves, a few blueberries, cucumber portions, apple chunks, lemon quarters, and a small piece of ginger.

eleven. Continue this layering method till all the factors had been juiced.

12. If the aggregate becomes too thick or difficult to juice, you could upload up to half of cup entire of water to advantage your preferred consistency.

13. Pour the freshly extracted spinach berry juice into glasses complete of ice cubes for a clean contact.

14. Optionally, you could garnish each glass with a strawberry or a lemon wheel for a in addition aesthetic enchantment.

Serving Total:

Kcal: eighty five

Carbs: 21g

Fats: 0.8g

Proteins: 2g

eighty four. Lemonic Turmeric Tonic

Preparation Period: 15 Min

Serves: 2

Ingredients favored:

2 large lemons

1 medium-sized clean turmeric root (about 2 inches)

1 small piece of easy ginger (about 1 inch)

2 tsp. Of honey (regulate to taste)

A pinch of black pepper

2 cups of cold water

Ice cubes (optionally available)

Fresh mint leaves or lemon slices for garnish (non-compulsory)

Preparation method

1. Begin with the useful useful resource of washing the lemons, turmeric root, and ginger under cold walking water to put off any dust or impurities.

2. Using a vegetable striper, gently strip the outer pores and pores and pores and skin of the lemons, avoiding the bitter white pith. Set aside the stripped lemons.

3. Cut the stripped lemons in half of of and dispose of any seeds. A citrus juicer or hand-held lemon reamer will make juicing less complicated.

4. Juice every lemons till you have got were given about 1/2 of cup (120ml) of sparkling lemon juice. Pour the lemon juice proper into a bowl and set it apart.

5. With a knife, carefully strip the turmeric root and ginger. Turmeric can stain, so deal with it with care to avoid staining your palms or decreasing board.

6. Cut the stripped turmeric and ginger into small, feasible portions. Smaller portions will mixture more without issue.

7. In a blender, combine the freshly squeezed lemon juice, turmeric, ginger, honey, and a pinch of black pepper. Black pepper enhances the absorption of curcumin, the active compound in turmeric.

8. Add 1 cup complete of bloodless water to the blender and blend the combination until it is straightforward and well blended. If you select a thinner consistency, you can add greater water to reap your preferred thickness.

nine. To dispose of any final solids and obtain a smoother texture, stress the mixture through a fantastic mesh strainer or cheesecloth right into a smooth bowl or pitcher.

10. Fill glasses with ice cubes if desired, and pour the freshly organized tonic over the ice.

11. Garnish with a fresh mint sprig or a slice of lemon for a touch of beauty and similarly flavor.

12. Serve proper now and enjoy your revitalizing Lemonic Turmeric Tonic.

Serving Total:

Kcal: 50

Carbs: 13 g

Fat: 0 g

Protein: 0.Five g

eighty five. Tart Cherry Bliss

Preparation Period: 20 Min

Serves: four

Ingredients wanted:

4 cups (approximately 1 lb.) entire of smooth or frozen tart cherries

half of cup entire of water (non-obligatory, for a thinner consistency)

1-2 tbsp. Complete of honey or maple syrup (non-compulsory, for sweetness)

1 lemon, juiced (non-compulsory, for introduced zing)

Preparation method

1. If the usage of clean cherries, start through washing them thoroughly and casting off the stems. You can use a cherry pitter to put off the pits, or you could do it via manner of hand. To pit cherries through hand, use a paring knife to make a small reduce across the cherry's circumference, then lightly twist and pull the pit out.

2. Blanching can assist soften the cherries and motive them to less difficult to juice. Bring a pot of water to a boil and punctiliously drop the cherries into the boiling water for approximately 30 seconds. Then, switch them to a bowl of ice water to cool speedy. Once cooled, drain the cherries.

3. You can use a juicer specifically designed for culmination or a amazing mesh strainer at the aspect of a spatula to extract the juice. If you're using a juicer, comply with the producer's instructions. If the usage of a strainer, location the blanched or glowing cherries in it, and use the decrease lower back of a spoon to press down and extract the juice. Collect the juice in a bowl, and set aside.

4. Taste the tart cherry juice and decide if you'd want to function sweetness. Depending on your preference, you can upload 1-2 tbsp. Complete of of honey or maple syrup. Stir nicely until the sweetener is virtually

dissolved. Additionally, you could upload sparkling lemon juice for a tangy twist.

five. If you discover the tart cherry juice too centered, you can add water to acquire your preferred consistency. Start through including half of of cup whole of water, then adjust further if wanted. Mix well.

6. Refrigerate the tart cherry juice till it's miles properly chilled. Serve it in a glass with ice cubes or revel in it as is.

Serving Total:

Kcal: one hundred ten

Carbs: 27 g

Fat: zero g

Protein: 2 g

86. Refreshing Pineapple Lemon Juice

Preparation Period: 15 Min

Serves: 2

Ingredients wanted:

1 medium-sized ripe pineapple

2 huge lemons

1 tbsp. Complete of honey (non-compulsory, for introduced sweetness)

Ice cubes (non-obligatory)

Fresh mint leaves for garnish (non-compulsory)

Preparation system

1. Place the pineapple on a reducing board and reduce off the pinnacle and backside just so it can stand upright.

2. With a pointy knife, carefully cut away the pores and pores and pores and skin, following the contour of the fruit from pinnacle to bottom. Make sure to put off all the prickly "eyes" on the ground.

three. Once the pores and skin is removed, stand the pineapple upright over again and reduce it into quarters lengthwise.

four. Each pineapple location has a difficult, fibrous center walking thru it. To take away it, role your knife at an thoughts-set and reduce along the center, reducing it far from the fruit.

5. Cut the pineapple quarters into small, chunk-sized chunks. You can alter the scale based totally absolutely surely in your choice. Larger chunks might also require a higher juicer.

6. Roll the lemons on the counter on the identical time as making use of mild strain. This will assist melt them and motive them to less complicated to juice.

7. Cut the lemons in half of and squeeze the juice using a citrus juicer or thru hand. Strain the lemon juice via a top notch-mesh sieve to cast off any seeds or pulp.

8. If you have got got a juicer, feed the pineapple chunks thru it to extract the sparkling pineapple juice. If you do not have a juicer, you may mixture the pineapple chunks

in a blender till smooth after which stress the aggregate through a exquisite-mesh sieve to collect the juice.

nine. In a tumbler, combine the freshly squeezed lemon juice and the pineapple juice. If you make a decision on a sweeter flavor, upload a tablespoon of honey and stir till it dissolves. Adjust the marvel in your liking with the aid of using which include more honey if preferred.

10. If you want your juice chilled, refrigerate it for about 30 Min or upload ice cubes to the pitcher in advance than serving.

11. Pour the pineapple lemon juice into glasses, garnish with clean mint leaves if favored, and serve right away.

Serving Total:

Kcal: one zero 5

Carbs: 28 g

Fat: zero.6g

Protein: zero.7g

87. Pineapple Almond Juice

Preparation Period: 15 Min

Serves: 2

Ingredients wished:

1 medium-sized ripe pineapple

1/2 of cup entire of raw almonds, soaked in a unmarried day and worn-out

1 tbsp. Complete of honey (non-obligatory, for brought sweetness)

1 cup entire of bloodless water

Ice cubes (non-compulsory)

Preparation approach

1. Lay the pineapple on its difficulty on a reducing board.

2. Using a pointy chef's knife, slice off the crown and the lowest of the pineapple.

three. Stand the pineapple upright and punctiliously cut away the pores and skin in a downward movement, following the natural curve of the fruit.

four. Once the skin is eliminated, you may see brown "eyes" scattered across the pineapple's flesh. To get rid of them, make a diagonal cut around the center, developing a spiral sample as you pass. Repeat till all of the eyes are eliminated.

5. Cut the pineapple into chunks, ensuring to put off the hard core from the middle of each piece.

6. Place the soaked almonds in a pleasing-mesh strainer and rinse them very well under bloodless walking water.

7. Drain the almonds honestly.

8. In a excessive-pace blender, integrate the pineapple chunks and worn-out almonds.

nine. Add 1 cup complete of bloodless water to the blender. If you select a sweeter juice, you can upload 1 tablespoon of honey at this degree.

10.   Blend the combination on immoderate speed until it becomes easy and creamy, typically for approximately 2-three Min. If the consistency is actually too thick, you could upload a piece more water and blend once more until you advantage your chosen texture.

11.   If making a decision upon a calming beverage, you could upload a handful of ice cubes to the blender and blend till they'll be certainly incorporated.

12.   While the juice is creamy and rich in fiber from the almonds, some may additionally moreover pick out a smoother texture. If so, strain the juice via a extraordinary-mesh strainer or nut milk bag right proper into a clean box or pitcher.

13.   Pour the pineapple almond juice into glasses.

14. Garnish with a pineapple wedge or a slice of smooth pineapple, if preferred.

15. Serve proper now and revel in the easy taste of this selfmade juice.

Serving Total:

Kcal: 220 c

Carbs: 40 g

Fat: 7 g

Protein: four g

88. Tomato Apricot Juice

Preparation Period: 20 Min

Serves: 2

Ingredients desired:

four ripe tomatoes

6 ripe apricots

1 small cucumber

1 small pink bell pepper

1 small lemon

1-inch piece of sparkling ginger

A pinch of salt (non-compulsory)

Ice cubes (non-compulsory)

Preparation approach

1. Start by the use of way of washing all the give up quit end result and veggies thoroughly.

2. Slice the tomatoes in half of and get rid of the green stems.

three. Cut the apricots in half of, doing away with the pits.

four. Strip the cucumber and cut it into chunks.

5. Remove the seeds and stem from the purple bell pepper and cube it into smaller portions.

6. Zest the lemon for delivered taste, after which juice the lemon to extract its juice.

7. Strip the ginger and dice it into small quantities.

8. To without trouble strip the tomatoes, you may blanch them. Boil a pot of water and put together a bowl of ice water.

9. Make a small "X" mark on the bottom of every tomato.

10. Carefully vicinity the tomatoes within the boiling water for about 30 seconds, or till you observe the skins begin to loosen.

eleven. Quickly switch the tomatoes to the ice water to take a seat returned.

12. Once cooled, strip off the tomato skins beginning from the "X" mark.

thirteen. Set up your juicer in line with the producer's commands.

14. Alternate between including small quantities of every component into the juicer to ensure even blending.

15. Start with tomatoes, then add apricots, cucumber, pink bell pepper, ginger, and lemon juice.

sixteen. If you select out a piece of saltiness in your juice, add a pinch of salt to taste.

17. Stir the juice gently to combine all the flavors.

18. If favored, add ice cubes to the juice to make it refreshingly cold.

Serving Total:

Kcal: 90 five kcal

Carbs: 23g

Protein: 3g

Fat: 0.7g

89. Elderberry Orange Juice

Preparation Period: 15 Min

Serves: 2

Ingredients wanted:

1 cup whole of clean elderberries (or frozen, thawed)

2 big navel oranges

1 tbsp. Complete of honey (non-obligatory, for added sweetness)

Ice cubes (non-compulsory, for a chilled beverage)

Preparation way

1. Begin with the aid of amassing all of the factors you could need: clean elderberries, navel oranges, honey (if the usage of), and ice cubes (if making a decision upon a calming drink).

2. If using easy elderberries, start with the resource of rinsing them thoroughly below cold water. Elderberries develop in clusters and are small, darkish red or black

berries. Remove any stems and leaves, leaving notable the berries.

3. Wash the navel oranges properly. Using a pointy knife, carefully lessen off the pinnacle and backside ends of each orange to create flat surfaces. This will make it simpler to strip and segment.

4. With the flat bottom of the orange resting in your decreasing board, use the knife to slice away the strip and pith in strips, following the curve of the fruit from pinnacle to bottom. Make fantastic to cast off all of the white pith, as it can be bitter.

5. Once stripped, preserve the orange over a bowl to seize any juice, and punctiliously lessen some of the membranes to release the orange segments. Allow the segments to fall into the bowl, leaving at the back of any seeds.

6. After segmenting the oranges, you can further extract the juice from the last membranes thru squeezing them over a

separate bowl or the use of a citrus juicer. This will maximize the orange taste in your juice.

7. Place the organized elderberries and orange segments (along aspect any extra juice you extracted) in a blender.

eight. If you make a decision upon a sweeter juice, add a tablespoon of honey to the blender.

nine. Optionally, add a handful of ice cubes for a sparkling chilled drink.

10. Secure the lid on the blender and mix the materials on immoderate velocity till the mixture will become easy and all the elderberries are nicely blanketed. This want to take about 1-2 Min.

Chapter 10: The Fascinating History

Welcome to a adventure thru the wealthy information of juicing, a practice that has now not simplest quenched our thirst for scrumptious drinks but has moreover nourished civilizations for hundreds of years. In this economic disaster, we will embark on a voyage lower returned in time to find out the origins and evolution of juicing, uncovering its captivating statistics.

Juicing isn't always most effective a modern-day health craze; it is a workout deeply rooted in human records. Our story starts offevolved offevolved offevolved in ancient civilizations, wherein people first found out the great ability of extracting liquid from end result and greens. The Egyptians, for instance, had been seemed to crush pomegranates and figs to create clean concoctions, at the identical time due to the fact the Chinese explored the advantages of the usage of bamboo tubes to extract juice from various vegetation.

Fast forward to the Middle Ages, and juicing have grow to be intertwined with alchemy, a precursor to modern generation. Alchemists, intrigued with the aid of manner of the transformative electricity of juicing, experimented with herbs and give up end result, searching for the elixir of existence. While their quest for immortality may not have succeeded, it fueled our facts of the medicinal houses of juices.

As the area entered the Age of Enlightenment, so did our know-how of nutrients. Pioneering scientists like Antoine Lavoisier started out to solve the chemical composition of ingredients, collectively with give up end result and greens. This newfound facts delivered approximately a deeper appreciation of juicing as a way to extract essential nutrients and vitamins.

During the early 20th century, the "Juice Movement" received momentum in the United States. Visionaries like Dr. Norman Walker pioneered the idea of juicing for health. His invention of the hydraulic press juicer allowed for the inexperienced extraction of juices, promoting power and properly-being. This marked a turning element, as juicing transitioned from a easy culinary exercising to a wellbeing revolution.

In present day a long term, juicing has skilled a renaissance, thank you in issue to the art work of influential figures like Jay Kordich, referred to as the "Juiceman." Their strength of will to promoting the benefits of clean juice sparked a renewed interest in juicing among health-aware individuals. With the arrival of modern juicers, it have grow to be less difficult than ever to encompass this exercise into every day lifestyles.

Today, juicing has transcended cultural and geographical barriers. It's now not constrained to notable health retreats but is embraced by using people from all walks of life, who're searching for to improve their desired fitness and power stages. The juicing motion keeps to expand, inspiring modern-day recipes, properly being programs, or maybe juice bars on every corner.

In the following chapters, we can delve deeper into the generation and benefits of juicing, addressing the very reasons why it subjects in your fitness. But earlier than we circulate beforehand, take a 2d to understand the historic tapestry that has introduced us up to now. Juicing, with its charming data, offers us now not best a taste of the beyond however a sip of the future, wherein fitness and energy are inner reap of all people.

The Power of Juicing: Why It Matters for Your Health

In the ever-evolving panorama of health and health, juicing has emerged as a powerhouse of energy, nourishment, and transformation. Beyond its scrumptious taste and colorful colors, the real magic of juicing lies in its profound effect for your health and properly-being. Let's discover why juicing subjects and the way it could emerge as a cornerstone of your journey in the path of a extra healthy life.

Juicing is a dynamic gateway to unlocking the powerful nutrients and vitamins hidden within give up end result and veggies. When you juice, you are essentially extracting the essence of these herbal wonders in liquid form. This manner that your body can take in those nutrients more efficaciously and successfully than via conventional ingesting. Take vitamins C, as an example. It's giant in citrus quit result like oranges and lemons. When you juice those fruits, you're freeing a focused burst of nutrition C that would bolster your immune device, improve collagen manufacturing for radiant pores and skin, or even beautify wound recovery. This is absolutely one instance of the nutritional treasure trove that juicing opens up.

Staying as it should be hydrated is important for preserving fitness and vitality. While water is vital, juicing gives a flavorful twist on your hydration regular. The water content in culmination and veggies isn't first-rate hydrating but additionally infused with vital minerals and electrolytes. Imagine sipping on a clean watermelon or cucumber juice on a scorching summer day. Not high-quality are you quenching your thirst, but you also are replenishing electrolytes like potassium, which aids in muscle characteristic and helps adjust blood pressure. Juicing gives a delectable and hydrating solution that maintains your electricity ranges immoderate.

In cutting-edge-day international, our our bodies are exposed to diverse environmental pollution and processed foods that can burden our gadget. Juicing acts as a natural detoxifier, assisting your frame cast off waste and threatening materials. The antioxidants and phytochemicals decided in plenty of end result and vegetables are like superheroes in your liver and kidneys, helping their detoxing functions.

Additionally, juicing can promote wholesome digestion. The fiber in entire quit end result and greens may be hard for a few to digest. When you juice, you eliminate the fiber, making it less complicated to your frame to soak up the vitamins with out taxing your digestive system. This can result in advanced intestine fitness, decreased bloating, and accelerated strength.

The nutrients and minerals in sparkling juice act as a natural electricity booster, revitalizing your body and mind. The aggregate of vital nutrients, antioxidants, and hydration in juice can improve cognitive characteristic, polishing your attention and highbrow clarity. Whether you're making ready for a demanding day at paintings or want a day pick out-me-up, a pitcher of sparkling juice can offer the sustained strength you need.

Juicing topics because it offers a transformative journey within the route of more fine health, accelerated power, and a colorful life. As you find out the pages of this e-book and embark on your very non-public juicing adventure, maintain in thoughts that the energy of juicing is not pretty much sipping a tasty beverage it's miles approximately harnessing the potential of nature to nourish your frame and revitalize your spirit.

Your Juicing FAQs Answered: Everything You Need to Know

Juicing can also appear to be a clean concept, but as you dive into this worldwide of colourful concoctions and health modifications, you are certain to have questions. We're proper proper here to answer your most urgent juicing FAQs and provide you with the expertise you need to embark in your juicing adventure with self guarantee.

What Exactly Is Juicing?

At its center, juicing entails extracting the liquid, or juice, from end result and veggies. This liquid includes the focused nutrients, minerals, and phytonutrients located inside the ones meals. Juicing gets rid of the fiber, making it less difficult in your frame to absorb those critical vitamins.

Why Juice When You Can Eat Whole Fruits and Vegetables?

Eating complete culmination and greens is undeniably critical. They offer fiber and a fulfilling crunch that juicing on my own can not reflect. However, juicing gives a completely particular benefit: it lets in you to consume a better amount and form of cease end result and greens in a single glass. This centered burst of nutrients may be especially useful for those striving to enhance their fitness and power stages.

Is Juicing a Replacement for a Meal?

While juicing can be a nutritious addition to your eating regimen, it's miles no longer typically advocated as a complete meal opportunity. Instead, think about it as a supplement to your present day food plan. A glass of sparkling juice may be an exquisite way to begin your day or a healthy snack amongst meals. Incorporating juicing into your daily recurring can beautify your selected nutrients.

What Types of Juicer Should I Use?

Choosing the proper juicer is vital. There are number one kinds: centrifugal juicers and masticating juicers (moreover called sluggish juicers). Centrifugal juicers are quicker but can also generate warm temperature which could lessen nutrient content material material. Masticating juicers perform at a slower pace and are greater green at extracting juice on the same time as preserving vitamins. Your choice is based upon to your price range and juicing possibilities.

Are There Any Specific Juicing Tips for Beginners?

Chapter 11: Embracing The Benefits Of Juicing

Juicing for Health: How It Boosts Your Well-Being

Juicing isn't only a modern-day health fad; it's far a effective elixir for enhancing your ordinary nicely-being. As you sip on that clean, vibrant juice, you are unlocking a international of blessings that enlarge a ways beyond the flavor. Let's delve into how juicing can revolutionize your fitness and growth your experience of properly-being.

One of the maximum super elements of juicing is its capacity to deliver a centered dose of vitamins for your body. When you eat a glass of glowing juice, you're flooding your device with nutrients, minerals, and antioxidants in their purest form. These critical factors play pivotal roles in supporting your health. For instance, eating regimen C, determined in abundance in citrus give up give up end result, is a effective antioxidant that strengthens your immune device, assisting you keep off illnesses. Meanwhile, diet A, determined in carrots and leafy veggies, promotes healthy vision, and allows skin fitness. The wealthy sort of vitamins in juices contributes to your regular energy and properly-being.

Gut Health and Digestive Harmony

A healthy intestine is the cornerstone of nicely-being. Juicing may be a mild but effective way to promote digestive health. The liquid nature of juice allows your frame to take in nutrients speedy and efficiently, lowering the pressure for your digestive gadget.

Additionally, many stop end result and vegetables utilized in juicing include herbal enzymes that useful useful resource digestion. These enzymes help in breaking down food, assuaging problems like bloating and pain. Regular juicing can make a contribution to a balanced and harmonious digestive system, leaving you feeling lighter and similarly energized.

They say beauty comes from inside, and juicing aligns perfectly with this concept. The immoderate content fabric of vitamins and antioxidants in sparkling juice can redesign your complexion, leaving your skin radiant and extra younger. Antioxidants fight the damaging results of free radicals, helping to slow down the developing vintage technique.

Vitamin E, determined in avocado and spinach juices, enables pores and skin restore and regeneration, contributing to a glowing complexion. Meanwhile, the hydrating homes of cucumber and watermelon juices can assist maintain pores and skin elasticity and decrease the arrival of top notch lines.

As you juice your way to higher fitness, you could possibly be aware the bonus of a complicated complexion.

Keep in thoughts the essence of our adventure: Integrating juicing into your every day existence for the sake of frequent properly-being. This is in which the enchantment of juicing honestly emerges.

Consistently indulging in fresh juices has the potential to bring about a exquisite surge to your strength degrees and an better sense of energy.

The vitamins and minerals in juice act as herbal energy boosters. They gas your cells, assisting your body characteristic at its best. When your cells are nourished and energized, you'll be aware a newfound energy for your day by day sports sports. Whether it is tackling a stressful workday or embarking on a circle of relatives journey, juicing can be your mystery weapon for sustained power.

Juicing is a journey to properly being, a direction in the course of a more in shape and greater colorful you. As you encompass the blessings of juicing, you may find out that it's far not quite an awful lot the elements you mixture; it's far about the transformation taking place within you. From superior digestion to radiant pores and skin, from extended strength stages to a profound sense of nicely-being, juicing is your rate tag to a greater healthy and happier life.

Energy and Vitality Unleashed: The Juicing Effect

In the hustle and bustle of modern-day life, keeping immoderate electricity tiers and a zest for dwelling is paramount. This is exactly in which juicing comes into its non-public, unraveling a international of vibrancy and strength that would invigorate your each day existence.

The very essence of juicing lies in its ability to infuse your body with revitalizing power. With every sip of easy juice, you're providing your device with a focused elixir of life. The nutrients and minerals determined in surrender end result and greens are similar to the fuel that powers your frame's engine. Take, as an instance, the dynamic duo of beetroot and kale. When juiced collectively, they create a robust aggregate rich in iron and antioxidants. This aggregate can beautify your body's oxygen-carrying ability, fight fatigue, and maintain your electricity ranges commonly excessive at some stage in the day.

For the ones striving for greater stamina and resilience, juicing is a venture-changer. The vitamins and phytonutrients placed in sparkling juice can bolster your frame's defenses in competition to the stresses of each day lifestyles. Whether it is handling a worrying hobby or keeping up with an active circle of relatives, juicing can offer the staying power you need. Imagine the rejuvenating strength of a spinach and pineapple juice. Spinach gives a wealth of vitamins, along side iron, on the identical time as pineapple contributes with bromelain, an enzyme appeared for its anti inflammatory homes. This mixture no longer handiest promotes established health but additionally fortifies your body's resilience to each day challenges.

In a global wherein coffee regularly takes center diploma due to the truth the circulate-to electricity booster, juicing offers a herbal possibility. The energizing consequences of glowing juice can rival that of your morning cup of joe without the caffeine-brought on jitters. Consider the invigorating combination of orange and carrot juice. Oranges bring a burst of vitamins C and natural sugars, providing a direct boom in strength. Carrots, instead, are full of antioxidants and beta-carotene, imparting sustained strength at a few level within the day. With juicing, you could revel in an power enhance this is both natural and enduring.

Energy isn't clearly about physical power; it's also approximately mental clarity and emotional stability. The vitamins in easy juice help cognitive feature, helping you stay centered and alert. Additionally, the influx of antioxidants can fight stress and sell a sense of emotional nicely-being. Picture a clean cucumber and mint juice. Cucumbers are hydrating and cooling, at the same time as mint offers a sparkling burst of flavor. This combination can leave you feeling each mentally invigorated and emotionally

Chapter 12: Essential Tools

Juicing Made Easy: Must-Have Kitchen Gear

Creating smooth and nutritious juices at home may be a breeze with the right equipment and device. Let's find out the crucial kitchen gear at the manner to make your juicing journey smooth and on hand.

1. High-Quality Juicer

Investing in a splendid juicer is the cornerstone of a hit juicing. Whether you decide upon a centrifugal, masticating, or cold-press juicer, pick out one which suits your desires and charge range. A proper juicer correctly extracts juice from culmination and greens, making sure you get the maximum vitamins from your factors.

2. Sharp Knives and Cutting Board

Preparation is essential to juicing. A set of sharp knives and a strong slicing board will make slicing and dicing end result and greens a breeze. Properly prepped additives ensure a clean juicing method and higher extraction of juice.

three. Citrus Juicer

For citrus enthusiasts, a dedicated citrus juicer is a have to. It simplifies the undertaking of extracting juice from lemons, limes, oranges, and grapefruits. Whether you are inclusive of a zesty twist to your juices or getting equipped citrus-primarily based definitely truly recipes, this tool is available in reachable.

four. Large Mixing Bowl

Having a spacious blending bowl accessible is wise for accumulating freshly juiced liquid and preventing any spills or messes. It's specifically beneficial whilst you are juicing large quantities or multiple elements.

five. Fine-Mesh Strainer

To advantage silky-smooth juice with out more pulp, a terrific-mesh strainer is your wonderful pal. It lets in get rid of any small debris and ensures a easy, diffused final product. This step is specifically favored at the identical time as you are serving juice to those who pick a pulp-free experience.

6. Glass Bottles or Jars

Storing your freshly made juice is crucial for retaining its freshness and nutritional fee. Glass bottles or jars with airtight lids are best for preserving your juices. They're additionally green and loose from risky chemical substances which can leach into your drinks. By assembling these want to-have kitchen tools, you may be properly-organized to embark on your juicing adventure with out a problem. The right device now not first-class streamlines the machine but additionally enhances the general juicing enjoy, making it a pleasant and available addition for your day by day routine.

Elevating Flavor: Adding Excitement to Your Juices

Juicing is not pretty plenty fitness; it's also about savoring the colourful and scrumptious flavors of glowing end result and greens. Elevate your juicing experience through using exploring severa elements and mixtures that upload delight in your juices.

Think of juicing as an opportunity to create a symphony of flavors on your glass. While conventional mixtures like apple and carrot are terrific, don't be afraid to test with surprising pairings. Try adding a slice of ginger for a distinctly spiced kick or a handful of glowing herbs like mint or basil for an fragrant twist. Achieving the right stability amongst candy and tart flavors may want to make your juices genuinely memorable. Citrus fruits like oranges and lemons supply a zesty tartness, even as surrender end result like apples and pineapples offer natural sweetness. Play with the ratios to find out your best concord of flavors.

Expand your horizons through the usage of incorporating awesome elements into your juices. Tropical culmination like mango, papaya, and ardour fruit can shipping your flavor buds to a long way-off locations. Explore the particular flavors of dragon fruit, lychee, or kiwi for a burst of tropical goodness. Herbs and spices are like magic wands in juicing, such as depth and complexity on your creations. Fresh basil can infuse a Mediterranean flair, while a pinch of cinnamon can evoke heat and comforting sensations. Experiment with those aromatic additives to find out your signature taste profile.

For a creamy and nutrient-rich twist, take into account including nut butters like almond or cashew to your juices. They impart a luscious texture and a hint of nutty goodness. Chia seeds or flaxseeds are super alternatives for a dose of healthful fat and brought thickness.

Edible vegetation like lavender, hibiscus, or rose petals can carry floral and fragrant notes in your juices. Not handiest do they decorate the visible appeal, however additionally they make a contribution particular flavors that tantalize the senses.

Juicing is your canvas, and the elements are your palette. Let your creativity waft as you check with special flavors and combos. Elevating the flavor of your juices offers an element of pride and adventure for your juicing adventure, making it a nice and scrumptious manner to encompass better health.

Exploring New Tastes: Unique Ingredients to Spice Up Your Juicing

Dive right right right into a worldwide of culinary journey with unique and surprising elements that could take your juicing experience to the subsequent level. These specific additions can spice up your juices and add a sprint of novelty to your every day everyday.

Root to Stem Juicing

Don't discard the regularly-unnoticed factors of give up result and vegetables. Try juicing root-to-stem to lessen food waste and maximize taste. Carrot vegetables, beet vegetables, and celery leaves are extraordinary examples. They provide a barely taken into consideration one in all a type flavor profile and provide an earthy, inexperienced essence to your juices.

Superfood Powders

Boost the dietary content cloth of your juices by using using the usage of incorporating superfood powders. Spirulina, wheatgrass, and moringa are electricity-packed options. They're rich in vitamins, minerals, and antioxidants, which includes a colorful inexperienced hue and a dietary punch to your concoctions.

Exotic Berries

While you is probably acquainted with strawberries and blueberries, consider exploring unique berries like goji, acai, or elderberry. These little gem stones are bursting with specific flavors and fitness advantages, making them a lovable addition in your juicing repertoire.

Unconventional Greens

Swap out your stylish spinach or kale for less commonplace greens like Swiss chard, arugula, or collard greens. They convey a extraordinary size of flavor and vitamins to your juices, making every sip a lovely and exceptional experience.

Savory Elements

Break a protracted manner from the splendor of traditional juices by way of together with savory factors like cucumber, bell peppers, or possibly a touch of chili. These substances create a harmonious balance and may lend a fresh and barely highly spiced be conscious for your drinks.

Herbal Elegance

Herbs are not best for garnish; they may be capable of boom your juicing activity. Try including herbs like parsley, cilantro, or thyme to infuse your juices with herbal splendor. Their fragrant characteristics and diffused flavors can complement a huge range of things.

Exploring new tastes in juicing is corresponding to embarking on a culinary journey. It's an opportunity to awaken your palate, discover interesting taste mixtures, and gain the blessings of a various array of vitamins. Embrace the sector of specific components and permit your flavor buds take satisfaction within the wonderful. Juicing is extra than first-rate a fitness adventure; it's far a scrumptious exploration of flavors and opportunities.

www.ingramcontent.com/pod-product-compliance
Lightning Source LLC
Chambersburg PA
CBHW071443080526
44587CB00014B/1971